Gentle
action

Bringing creative change
to a turbulent world

F. David Peat

Gentle
action

Bringing creative change
to a turbulent world

Pari
Publishing

For Hannah

"David Peat is one of those rare authors who can consistently blend scientific curiosity with emotional insight and compassion. The ideas and analogies contained in this book are both powerful and compelling. His gift for skillfully layering complex thoughts with subtle, crisp reasoning brings theoretical physics to the mainstream in a way that will leave you spellbound."

Mark Adams, author, *The Elements of Transformation*

"The key question for any responsible person in this world beset with so many staggering problems is: what can I do? David Peat has written a most timely and inspiring book. In *Gentle Action* he shares with us not only valuable insights about how to act but provides us also with a rich array of people who took a stand and made a difference.
This encouraging book should be widely read!"

Edy Korthals Altes, former Ambassador of the Netherlands; former Co-President World Conference of Religions for Peace (WCRP)

"David Peat's acute analysis of human behavior and mechanistic systems, as seen through the eyes of a physicist, is both fascinating and insightful. His perspective on the historical interplay between arts and science during the Renaissance seems particularly relevant in considering man's influence on today's turbulent world. Above all, this book highlights the curse of unintended consequences which can arise from ill-thought out interventions in our society and environment. If nothing else, read the story of the Nile perch. This and other pertinent case studies are shocking examples of what can happen when we fail, in David's words, to take gentle action or dance with nature."

Geoffrey Bush, Chairman, Diageo Foundation

"If you read only one book about how to contribute to positive change in your world today, choose *Gentle Action* by physicist turned philosopher F. David Peat. As usual, he has found a way to link abstract, yet pervasive qualities of human nature and the physical universe with practical approaches to making a difference."

Marguerite M. Callaway, President, Callaway Group, LLC, an international management consultancy. Author, *The Energetics of Business: A Practical guide to bringing your business to life*

"David Peat takes his deep life experience as a physicist, systems thinker, teacher, social entrepreneur and philosopher distilling what he has learned as a gift to our future. *Gentle Action* embraces positive change toward a sustainable world, showing in many fascinating stories, how each of us can contribute to healthier communities and societies."

Hazel Henderson, author, *Ethical Markets: Growing the green economy*

"F. David Peat has written perhaps his most important book, one that is required reading for those aspiring to address society's most complex and pressing issues. Peat's approach is both practical and elegant. It calls for subtle but significant action, consistent with natural principles, producing radical whole system transformation."

Joseph Jaworski, Generon International. Author, *Synchronicity: The inner path of leadership*

"*Gentle Action* gives hope in the face of the most common sources of powerlessness—the feeling that nothing can be done and that there are no resources to do it. In this intriguing book David Peat shows how with courage, intelligence, engagement and sensitivity we can help problems speak for themselves and suggest their own solution."

Graham Leicester, Director, International Futures Forum

"I enthusiastically endorse David Peat's book Gentle Action as a primer in the field of whole systems healing. The concept of gentle action has a key role to play, as it offers the framework for translating theory into action. In short, it is wonderfully useful!"

John Miller, External fellow, University of Minnesota, Founder and President of the forthcoming Albert Schweitzer College

"*Gentle Action* is profound and yet...gentle. It doesn't beat people up with an intellectual stick. Reading the book is like going to visit David Peat in Pari; it is an invitation to stop, rest, think and have a chat with fellow travelers and residents alike. Over food, of course, and wine...both made locally, by people who care."

Ernesto Sirolli, author, *Ripples from the Zambezi: Passion, entrepreneurship and the rebirth of the local economy*

"The damage we have done to our planet cannot be reversed by more of the same heavy, violent and invasive work. The system needs to evolve more subtly to stop this destruction. It is one thing to 'think' this—but even then, to stop the damage, the notion needs to be experienced 'outside' normal 'thought'. David Peat knows that these changes must emerge from *Gentle Action*. His book is an example of his action. It can help us save the Planet."

Lord Stone of Blackheath, Chairman of DIPEx a health charity, and Deputy Chairman of Sinicatum Carbon-Capital, a climate change company

"F. David Peat is an uncommon philosopher/physicist—he provides a theoretical framework, based in general systems theory, that brings the ideas of Mahatma Gandhi and Albert Schweitzer into the 21st century, making them relevant, practical and accessible. He's leading the way to a greener, kinder kind of engaged social action. Onward!"

Eric Utne, founder, *The Utne Reader*

"I have long lived by the dictum that we should in public life try to get as far as possible to the right-hand side of the following scale:

done to → done for → done with → done by

But never before have I had so clear a statement of why that should be the case as David Peat's *Gentle Action* provides."

Perry Walker, Head, Democracy and Participation, New Economic Foundation

"Too many change initiatives use control and fear, only creating more chaos. David Peat, with his always keen and discerning mind and heart, offers us real wisdom for how we can respond to turbulence in ways that create real possibilities and affirm life."

Margaret J. Wheatley, author, *Leadership and the New Science*

Pari Publishing

Via Tozzi 7, 58045 Pari, Grosseto, Italy
www.paripublishing.com

Table of Contents

Introduction.
Helping and trying to help

I'd like to begin this book on Gentle Action with two stories about people who attempted to improve a social situation by making an intervention. The first involves Ernesto Sirolli, who as a young man volunteered with the Italian Agency of Technical Cooperation, an aid agency working in Africa. Sirolli was one of five volunteers sent to a tiny village in Zambia with the intention of starting a farming project for the local inhabitants.[1] The long-term goal was to create a cooperative with shared tractors, seed and storage sheds. The first step towards this goal was to hire thirty local men to clear land in preparation for the farm. At the end of the first day things looked promising, and the men were paid the equivalent of one dollar; a sum agreed upon by the Zambian government and the Agency. On the second day no one turned up for work. It did not take long for the Italians to discover that one day's wage was sufficient to keep a family for a week, and so the question arose—how to persuade the men to turn up each morning, when they really did not need the extra money. The answer lay in some of the things the volunteers had brought with them—sunglasses, beer, whiskey, watches and transistor radios. They would persuade the workers to keep coming back each day until they had saved enough money to buy these objects.

And so the fields were cleared and crops of tomatoes planted with seeds brought from Italy. The whole project looked as if it was going to be an amazing success, for the Zambian soil and climate was producing gigantic plants. Finally, when the crop was almost ripened, Sirolli went out to view the fields. To his horror the tomatoes were nowhere to be seen. The culprits lay in the river—at night hippopotamuses had climbed onto the land and eaten all the tomatoes. No one had thought of the hippos. The project was an utter failure. All that had been achieved was to make the local people dependent on money and alcohol.

Sirolli looked around at what some of the other countries had been doing to "help" Africa and found several of their efforts to be equally well meaning but stupid—the donation of snow removal equipment to an airport in a region where it had never snowed; a supply of thousands of solar-powered ovens to people who traditionally cooked only at night. All of which reminds me of the way my Native American friends would joke that the worst thing they could hear is "We're from the government.

We've come to help you". Of course it must be said that not all people attempting to give aid abroad are that stupid. When a group of Italian businesspeople wished to help street children in Vietnam, they decided that it would make far more sense to teach them the skills needed to set up small businesses, such as bicycle repair, rather than handing out charity.[2]

The second story concerns Claire and Gordon Shippey, a young couple from Middlesbrough in the northeast of England who visited Pari in 2001 to take part in one of our courses.[3] (Pari is a medieval village located some 25 km south of Siena. In 1996 I moved to Pari from Canada and four years later set up the Pari Center for New Learning where we run conferences and offer courses.)

Middlesbrough used to be home to the type of traditional heavy industries (chiefly engineering and steel) that all but disappeared during the tumultuous Thatcher era. The city now faced chronic problems of unemployment, crime, drugs, and the disintegration of community. Some parts of the city, in particular where Claire and Gordon lived, were plagued with garbage-strewn areas with abandoned and burnt-out cars; places no longer safe for children to play outdoors. Indeed in October 2007 the British TV show *Location, Location, Location* still rated Middlesbrough as the worst place to live in the United Kingdom![4]

While in Pari, Claire and Gordon noticed that people left their keys in the front door, gathered in the piazza to talk and greeted each other by name. "I felt ashamed," Gordon said, "when I think our block is only half the size of Pari, yet we didn't even know each other's names. What hit me most and changed the way I felt about my hometown was when David showed us a video of Pari's *sagra* (the annual September festival). We could see the way that people had worked together." That night the couple did not sleep but spent hours discussing what they had been experiencing in the village. In such a short time, they had made friends with other people on the course, yet felt strangers in their own hometown.

Once they got home the Shippeys decided to make a change in their community through a very simple act. After work Gordon walked down their street, knocked on each door saying "I'm your neighbor, my name is Gordon Shippey." (Claire's night shift work prevented her joining him.) Then, together with two other neighbors, Nassian Hussian and Jason Stead, they decided to form a local group they called TAMS (Talbot Street/Alleys/Marton Road/Southfield Road—the streets most badly in need of community action).

Claire and Gordon were living five minutes from the city centre in a traditional working class area of row housing with back alleyways separating the rows of houses. Neither they nor their neighbors had any experience of political activism, nor did they have friends in high places, yet by bonding together they were able to bring about important changes in their community. With their community association, TAMS, the local people could make themselves be heard and tackle the problems they faced.

For example, residents from outside the immediate area had been dumping garbage in the shared back alleys between the rows of houses. TAMS therefore decided to made a video and photo account of the state of the alleys in order to stir the city council into action. Included in this display were cartoons drawn by local children presenting the problems through their own eyes, particularly the drug dealing that took place in the back alleys. As a result, the council agreed to put up gates to block traffic coming into the area and generally prevent unwanted outsiders from gaining access. The group also cleaned up an abandoned woodwork shop that had been used for drug dealing and applied for a grant to use it as offices.

As Gordon later wrote to me, "After we formed the TAMS Association, people began to talk to each other and children started to play outside. An older lady (89) said that the last time she saw this kind of thing round here was 35 years ago. We have met with local government officials and police and, as a collective, we have managed to push forward our idea of turning our burnt-out alleys into places where we can live and have parties. We have put forward other proposals, such as hanging baskets of flowers and blocking off the main road. We are now at the point of changing the area into a kind of village within a town. We had a good response from the shops in the area and the University of Teesside are willing to work with us as a number of houses are rented by students. Also the Member of Parliament for the area was impressed with the number of people who turned out to our meeting."

Two stories about local communities. Two solutions offered and two outcomes. What is so important about the difference between them? The answer if fairly obvious. The first example is one of thousands upon thousands of cases where a plan or policy is applied from outside, by people who don't really understand all the subtleties of living and working within a particular context or community. The second is a gentle, direct and creative approach, simply knocking on doors and giving one's name, and one devised by people who lived within a community, who wanted to make a tiny change for the better, and who ended up totally transforming the area in which they lived.

The question is, how do we go from the former way of thinking and acting, which is so deeply ingrained in our culture, to the latter? How do we move from policies, plans and "solutions" that are imposed on a situation, to a more intelligent and harmonious transformation that evolves out of the system itself?

This need to change our approach was the lesson learned by Sirolli in Zambia. He realized that imposing a solution from outside may not solve a problem but if, on the other hand, you listen to the local people they will let you know what needs doing. In any community, he believes, there will be at least one or two people who, if you put them together, will come up with the solution to the particular problem facing that community. Sirolli calls this Enterprise Facilitation. From now on Sirolli would send a facilitator into a town that had asked for help and wait for people to come to him or her, rather than the other way around. He was willing to help them with such practical matters as filling out forms and applications for permissions, but he would not offer them money or advice—both of which can rob people of self-sufficiency.

Where do we go from here?

At this point I'd like to anticipate some of the arguments of the book and briefly summarize why, even with the best of intentions, things can go so easily wrong.

- We feel uncomfortable when we are surrounded by uncertainty.

- We want to remain in control, so that when things do not go according to plan, we believe we must intervene.

- Our interventions, while based on good motives, may be grounded within a distorted perception of the situation in question. Our vision may be limited or prejudiced, and the system we are dealing with may be far more complex or delicate then we have anticipated.

- The basis from which we operate—the nature of a policy, organization, group or system of government—may be limited and over-rigid.

- The result is that the solution imposed, may be inappropriate and the degree of action taken disproportionate.

How can this state of affairs be changed? In this short book we shall examine an alternative. In essence this involves an initial "creative suspension" of action, with the aim of developing a clearer perception of the situation in hand, and then creating a basis for action that is more sensitive, flexible and creative. Out of these conditions will flow a more appropriate and harmonious action. This overall process I have termed "Gentle Action".

Notes

1. Ernesto Sirolli, *Ripples from the Zambezi: Passion, entrepreneurship, and the rebirth of local economies* (Gabriola Island, Canada: New Society Publishers, 1999).

2. Discussions with Giorgio Nelli, Civitella-Paganico.

3. The story of Claire and Gordon Shippey was gathered from my many conversations and email exchanges with them. Additional information can be found at www.paricenter.com/library/papers/gentle03.php.

4. http://channel4.com/4homes/ontv/location/index.html.

Chapter 1.
Living in a clockwork world

Gentle action was the approach taken by Claire and Gordon Shippey in Middlesbrough. It is the basis of Ernesto Sirolli's Enterprise Facilitation. But the Shippeys and Sirollis of this world are few and far between.* Most others who wish to "help", end up imposing solutions of their own making upon situations they may not fully understand. Why should this be? The answer, I believe, is that we apply approaches that, while they are successful in a number of limited cases, are not really appropriate to all the subtleties and complexities of most real-life situations.

The mechanistic approach can be incredibly successful when applied in the right context. Take for example an automobile. If it does not function properly you take it to a service station where a read-out is made from its internal computer. But this is a relatively recent innovation and for many decades human mechanics could quickly trace the fault and repair or replace the malfunction without the help of a computer. They knew that the engine works because the spark plugs fire at exactly the right moment when the mixture of air and gasoline is compressed in the cylinder. So the first thing to check is to see if the plug is making a spark. If it is not then the problem must lie somewhere between the battery and the plug. Are the battery connections tight? Is the distributor clean and dry?

But if the plug fires correctly then the problem must be in the other pathway, from gasoline tank to the cylinder and so the mechanic checks the carburetor. Maybe a needle valve is blocked? Step by step the source of the engine failure can be traced to a fault in an individual component. Getting the car running again involves cleaning, repairing or replacing the part that proved faulty.

---

*Or at least that is what I believed when I started to write this book but, via a blog I have been running, I have discovered a number of individuals who have been creating their own small acts of Gentle Action.

When it comes to engines and machines this approach is extremely powerful. It allows a complicated system to be analyzed into a series of separate interacting parts until the solution to any malfunction focuses on a particular faulty component. Machines can be analyzed in this way and the outcome of an intervention can be clearly predicted. How simple it would be if the same technique could be applied to the global problems that face us today; to economics, ecology, human conflict and even to our bodies. The difference is that nature, society and we ourselves are not machines but are enormously more complex and subtle, so behavior cannot be analyzed, evaluated or predicted in any mechanical way.

Admittedly doctors do successfully diagnose diseases, but they do not work in quite the same way as automobile mechanics. Determining a disease involves piecing together a complex set of signs and symptoms—a process that is closer to recognizing the features of a familiar face than the analysis of the parts of a machine. And recognizing faces is a highly sophisticated process on the part of the brain. We can spot a friend in a crowd after many years, under a variety of lighting situations, and even with different facial hair. No one yet fully understands how this is done, but we do know that recognizing faces and patterns of illnesses is far more complex than working with machines. In addition, although people "have" measles or influenza, the course of the particular illness is unique to each individual. Finally, while a medical solution may be proposed, just as a car is repaired, the actual course of the cure is not so predictable.

Our everyday experience tells us that nature and society are very definitely not mechanistic, but the problem is that in many ways we continue to behave as if they were. Our organizations often react in mechanical ways, and legislators believe that all problems should have well defined solutions, so that every situation must be exhaustively analyzed and the outcome of a course of action accurately predicted. When we view nature and society in this manner, as if it were an elaborate machine, we tend to act and treat them in a mechanical way. Therein lies the trouble. That, in essence, is why the world today faces so many problems and why the solutions offered by organizations and governments often do not work, or even end up making a situation much worse.

The origins of this way of approaching the world, I believe, can be traced back to the early Middle Ages.[1] Up to that point Europeans had lived in a universe that appeared alive to them. The world was ripe with connections, "sympathies" and correspondences. Metals were generated in the womb of the earth and the alchemist, artist, miner and metalworker were the midwives to nature, assisting her in her striving for perfection. Humans lived within the cycles of time and in a social space that was as rich as an egg. But during the second half of the 13th century, new technological inventions suddenly appeared. These were, in essence, powerful tools to aid abstract thinking.

Just as a lever enables people to lift a rock many times their own weight, so these tools of the mind enabled medieval people to arrange, manipulate, move and control their environment from within the world of thought. And, as thought manifested its power to manipulate a world of abstractions, so too their perception of the external, physical world began to transform and take on a new shape. The result was an accelerated journey towards our modern age of science and technology.

Human consciousness was learning how to transform the world and, in turn, this new world demanded more and more thought. The impact of these tools for thought was far more radical than the modern information revolution with its computers and the Internet. In fact the seeds of our own information revolution were sown almost eight hundred years ago!

What were these mental tools? They involved the ability to picture and represent the world through abstractions within the mind. Set below they don't look all that dramatic but their potential proved to be staggering. They included:

- The adoption of the Indo-Arabic number system instead of Roman numerals. (This made it much easier to add, subtract, divide and multiply large numbers.)

- The appearance of mechanical clocks on public buildings and the numerical measurement of time.

- The refinement of philosophical argument into a series of well defined logical steps.

- Double entry bookkeeping.

- Accurate map making.

- Systematic navigation.

Take, for example, the combination of double entry bookkeeping with Arabic numerals. Before these innovations, keeping track of a business was very much a hit-and-miss affair, one in which people never really knew the extent to which they were making a profit or loss. In place of business ledgers were anecdotal accounts of trade. But now, with these new tools, merchants could keep an accurate record of their profits and losses. They could calculate, for example, if it made economic sense for them to invest in a ship sailing to the Spice Islands. In this way merchants could create an image of the future and bring it into the present. They could make predictions. They had an increased measure of control over the economic world that surrounded them. What is more, time itself had been reduced to number. In the past, the church fathers had argued that usury (lending money with interest—in other words charging interest against the length of time the money is borrowed) was wrong because time belongs to God. But now time had been secularized and along with it came a new set of metaphors, such as "time is money", "saving time", "wasting time", "putting time aside", "investing time in...".

Incidentally, the early Middle Ages also saw the invention of the loom. In the nineteenth century Charles Babbage and his assistant, Augusta Lee, recognized that the way a loom reproduced the pattern of a carpet was because a sequence of actions had been programmed onto punched cards fed into the loom. Observing this they were struck with the idea of also weaving numbers. Out of this was born the notion of the computer and the computer program. The world had to wait for the advent of electronics before Babbage's dream could be turned into a reality, but the computer itself is no more than a creative unfolding of ideas and technologies laid down centuries earlier. In this, and in so many other ways, the foundation of all our modern science and technology was implicit within the transformation of consciousness that took place during the Middle Ages.

This period brought many triumphs but it also gave rise to a particular way of seeing the world that, in certain circumstances, can end up having disastrous effects. It was this new ability to envision the world as something outside ourselves, as something that can be controlled, predicted and manipulated, rather than as a living extension of ourselves and our society, that held a danger. And along with this new vision also came the dream of endless progress and increase.

Not long after this period Europe saw the rise of the Renaissance when the living world was further distanced from us and "Man" became the measure of all things. And what is the great invention associated with the Renaissance? Perspective in painting.

What is perspective? It is the world portrayed as being external to us. It is the world as seen by a one-eyed person whose head is clamped in a fixed position. It may produce a powerful illusion of external reality, but it is certainly very far from the way the eye and brain actually "see" the world, which is a highly active and intentional process.

Moreover, perspective gathers the world into a single logical scheme (technically this is called projective geometry) in which each individual object is distorted until it is made to fit the overarching mathematical logic. The circular openings of bowls now become ellipses, the walls of houses are no longer parallel to each other, roads appear to narrow in the distance. It was only with Cézanne that painting finally began to overthrow perspective and allow us to see each object, each of Cézanne's apples, as it really is.

Not long after the Renaissance came the rise of science, with Descartes, Galileo and Newton. Newton's contribution was of the greatest importance, for he produced the most successful theory hitherto seen; one that would unify so many different phenomena, from the fall of an apple to the orbit of the moon, under just three laws of motion. But this was done at a cost, for the universe of physics became nothing more than Newtonian clockwork. It was a universe without purpose. Earth was just one planet orbiting a perfectly ordinary star towards the edge of one galaxy amongst countless others. Life was a chemical accident. Pretty soon Nietzsche and others were writing about the Death of God.

Scientists (particularly physicists) sometimes claim that physics is the queen of the sciences. So according to them chemistry can be reduced to physics and, in turn, biology reduced to chemistry. Even Sigmund Freud believed that the mind would one day be understood "scientifically", and his theories of psychopathology were based upon the idea of blocks in the free flow of biological energy. Consciousness was reduced to thermodynamics! And if an objectified, reductionist approach could be applied to human behavior then why not to economics, history and sociology? Would all human knowledge one day be reduced to a single overarching scientific system? But here the problem begins, for when such a science objectifies nature and society and views it as a machine, albeit a highly subtle and complex machine, it leaves no room for human feelings and ethical values. It is a quantative science that gives no account of qualities.

While our everyday human experience tells us that this type of reductionist and mechanistic approach is not just over optimistic but in fact profoundly wrong, our organizations and governments, our plans and strategies, retain a simple faith in prediction and control. Clearly if, at its deepest level, the world is not mechanical, while our strategies and plans continue to be predicated upon a mechanical perspective, then we are bound to get into serious trouble. Mistaking the red light of a stop signal for a neon advertising sign may lead to a traffic accident. But looking at the problems of a rain forest, inner city violence, or the human body as if they are readily analyzable, to the point where we can obtain single solutions with predictable outcomes, is going to land us in even deeper trouble. Perceiving and valuing society, economies and nature in inappropriate ways has brought us to the series of crises the whole planet now faces.

The Newtonian or mechanical approach, when it is transferred from where it properly belongs to society, human interactions, and living environments, acts to oversimplify and fragment situations to the point where it may leave out what is most important. In addition, its power to create models, make precise calculations and produce predictions lures us into the false sense of security that we actually know what we are doing. Science has certainly increased our knowledge of the cosmos and has produced many technological miracles. On the other hand, two hundred years of scientific analysis and prediction has encouraged our objectification of the world, one that has had the effect of neglecting human values and weakening our relationship to nature. It has enhanced our tendency to dominate, control and exploit the world around us. Every problem, it is believed, has a solution that can be applied to a particular part of the system. And if that solution does not work, then yet another study group must be convened and its proposals applied with even greater vigor. Yes, we may face a series of crises, including global warming, but somehow, we believe, science and technology will come up with the solution so that we can go on behaving as we have done before. Objectifying nature leads to a loss of sensitivity and to a lack of meaning at our being "in the world".

Today we are becoming increasingly aware of the inadequacies of this traditional approach. There is the pragmatic objection that despite the policies and strategies of the past two hundred years our planet, and indeed human life, is now under such great threat that something must be fundamentally wrong with our relationship to the world. But it is also possible to attack a mechanistic, reductionist perspective on purely scientific grounds. Quantum theory, for example, shows us that, at the atomic level, nature cannot be broken into independent parts. Neils Bohr, one of the great prophets of quantum theory, spoke of a quantum system as being an unanalyzable whole. John Bell has demonstrated the curious correlation that exists between quantum systems, even when they are separated by large distances. Moreover Bell's correlations cannot be explained by appeal to any mechanical interaction. David Bohm termed his own approach to quantum theory as Bohmian non-mechanics. Nevertheless the mechanistic view of nature, as something external to us and constructed out of separate parts, like pieces of Lego, still holds an enormous sway over our minds. It is this mechanistic approach that is causing so many problems. This is why we need to replace our traditional responses with something new, with what I am calling Gentle Action. During the twentieth century, the traditional approach to science encountered hubris in the form of chaos theory and quantum theory. We moved from certainty to uncertainty. And now the new sciences are pointing the way to a new form of "gentle action".

Your reflections

At the end of each chapter this book poses a number of questions for the reader's reflection. The intention is to encourage you, the reader, to think about your own situation, at work and at home; and about the city, town or village in which you live, how your community functions, and how it connects to the larger world. It also invites you to explore issues that fascinate or concern you and asks in what ways are you making—or can you make in the future—an impact on, or influence, those around you.

After having read these sections you may like to share your reflections with others by posting you comment, observation or question on www.gentleaction.org.

  ∾ **Reflections on Chapter 1**

1. In the early Middle Ages people felt themselves to be an integral part of nature and to be living within the cycles of time. How do you experience the environment around you? And what about the passage of time? Is it only something measured by your wristwatch or do you experience time in other, "felt" ways?

2. If you live in the countryside you may feel an intimate connection to nature and the cycles of the day and seasons. How does that express itself in your daily life? But what if you live in the city? Is nature something you only experience on vacation or at the weekend? Or can you also discover a link to the living world amongst the streets, traffic and buildings?

3. In which cases have you found it helpful to carry out a "scientific" analysis of a particular system, a situation or a problem you face, by dividing it into a number of simpler parts that all interact together? And under what situations does this approach simply not work?

Notes

1. Additional information on the dramatic changes of the early Middle Ages can be found in Alfred W. Crosby, *The Measure of Reality: Quantification and Western society, 1250-1600* (Cambridge: Cambridge University Press, 1997).

Chapter 2.
Complexity and complication

Being in control

As we saw in the previous chapter, there is a pervading tendency within organizations to view the world in mechanistic ways and to desire certainty, predictability and control. Added to this is the belief, only relatively recently demolished, that we can enjoy endless progress within an infinitely abundant world. The first Europeans to encounter the New World, for example, saw a vast country of endless possibilities. And the doctrine of "manifest destiny" asserted that settlers had the inalienable right to push their way across that land from ocean to ocean.

I have some hint of what it may have been like to see a limitless land. I was born and brought up in a suburb of Liverpool and knew an environment that was crowded with people and buildings. Then, during the 1960s, I moved to Canada and realized I had come to a world of great open spaces. Canada appeared to extend forever. But that vision was shattered when one day as I sat on the shore of Lake Ontario—a lake so large you could almost drop England into it. A scuba diver surfaced near to where I was sitting and we began to talk. It turned out that he was a marine biologist looking for specific organisms. When I asked him why he told me that they were direct evidence that the lake was dying. At the time I found that incredibly hard to believe. I felt I was in a virgin land of clean air and water. Now I was told that human activity was killing the Great Lakes.

I should already have been warned, for Rachel Carson's book *Silent Spring*[1] had appeared in 1962 and was an important stepping-stone in the environmental movement. Eleven years later E. F. Schumacher's *Small is Beautiful*[2] sensitized us to the notion of sustainable development. And in the years that followed we would learn that the earth's resources are finite, that our use of fossil fuels cannot continue indefinitely. Moreover, the burning of these fossil fuels was increasing the amount of carbon dioxide in the atmosphere which, in turn, was causing global warming.

In the previous chapter science was portrayed as something of a villain, since it had presented us with a highly persuasive picture of the world as mechanistic, a picture which we had too easily transferred to our view of human society and even, with Freud, to the behavior of the individual. But science and its accompanying technology have also alerted us to the issues of global warming, global dimming* and the fragility of the ozone layer. Likewise, the technology of the space race produced a striking image—earth as a blue ball seen from space. It was this vision of our earthly habitat that became deeply symbolic for many people: This is our home and we must care for it.

Chaos theory

Science in the twentieth century also came up with another powerful conceptual image that acts to counteract that of the Newtonian clockwork. Its name is chaos theory and it has been applied widely to everything from the fluctuations of the stock market, to the spread of rumors, the fluctuations of populations, precursors of a heart attack, the growth of clouds, and so on.[3]

Whereas the science of previous centuries had sought to simplify the world, reducing it to interacting parts somewhat similar to the example of the faulty automobile, the science of chaos theory envisions the many systems surrounding us—natural, economic and social—as rich and varied landscapes containing hills, valleys, plains, mountain peaks, ridges and swamps. And while science of the previous eras could only be properly applied to such well defined systems as the flight of cannonballs, small flows of heat, weak currents of electricity and physical systems that were more or less in balance and did not change too rapidly, chaos theory had vastly wider applications. It describes such things as fractures in metals, noise in electrical amplifiers, tidal waves and vortices in rivers. But it also applies to such diverse systems as Jupiter's Red Spot and the rings of Saturn, the activities of the marketplace, weather systems, the classification of coastlines, fluctuations in the population of Arctic foxes

---

* Global dimming occurs when tiny water droplets condense around microparticles from pollutants in the upper atmosphere. The effect is to reduce the amount of sunlight reaching the earth's surface. In this way global dimming acts to reduce the effect of global warming and James Lovelock in his recent book, *The Revenge of Gaia*,[4] even suggests that global dimming should be enhanced by adding sulfur to aviation fuels. The disadvantage of global dimming, however, is that scientists believe it reduces the amount of water sucked up from the world's oceans with a consequent reduction in rainfall. Some fear that it could even compromise the monsoons that irrigate India, producing drought and starvation on a very large scale.

and even the creation of computer-generated planets for science fiction films.

All in all it is something of a miracle that so many vastly different phenomena can be collected within the one umbrella of chaos theory. And its most important lesson for us is that hitherto we had seen the world around us in over simplistic ways and had been gripped by the illusion that we were the drivers of the world, the ones truly in control. Rather than dancing with nature and engaging in a conversation with the world, we had constantly been trying to shout it down, for we had become inebriated with the sound of our own voices. Chaos theory taught us the hubris of that position and demoted us from our position of pride in our own abilities.

There are a number of lessons given to us by chaos theory that are of particular importance when considering Gentle Action. One is that natural and social systems are far more complex than we may have first considered. In fact, some of them are so complex that there will always be a degree of "missing information" in their description. No matter how well we study such systems, and how much data we collect, there will always be elements of the system that escape us. Put all your data in the world's biggest computer and you will still not be able to fully describe the system.

Another factor is that while, in some regions of behavior, it may be perfectly possible to predict the future of a system, in other areas its behavior may contain an element of uncertainty and unpredictability. Scientists refer to this as "extreme sensitivity to initial conditions". This means that if you don't have complete and accurate knowledge of the system at one point in time, then your prediction rapidly goes awry. But we have also learned that in some cases totally accurate knowledge about a system is not possible—the result is that in some situations we just have to accept uncertainty about the future and that is a very uncomfortable situation for some people and for many organizations.

Rapid changes are taking place all around us. These include globalization; developments in technology; fears of terrorism; mass migrations; the instability of the Middle East and parts of the Third World; the rise of the Pacific Rim, China and a United Europe; the breakdown of inner cities; economies that appear to be out of control with the consequent challenges of inflation, recession and unemployment; spiralling health costs; revolutions in communication technology and information processing; the demands of consumers and the lobbying of special interest groups; threatened species and ecologies; the dangers of global warming and ozone depletion; increasing rates of teenage suicide and drugs use; the transformation of management and the breakdown of conventional institutions. Governments, institutions, organizations and individuals experience considerable anxiety in the face of such rapid change and feel powerless to ameliorate the problems that surround them. Indeed, it sometimes appears as if their plans and policies, as well as the traditional structures of institutions, are themselves part of the problem.

In so many cases policies, plans, interventions and other actions, all taken in good faith, have not only failed to resolve an existing situation but in some cases have acted to magnify and render the problem even more intractable. In other cases, the attempt to impose a solution in one location, or context, has had the effect of creating an even larger problem elsewhere.

When organizations and individuals feel control slipping from their grasp, their natural reaction is to become even more intransigent in their attempt to clamp down on events and exert ever more control. The result is a spiral of control that has literally gone out of control! The realization that plans and policies are ineffective leads to a sense of depression and hopelessness. Faced with the insecurities and flux of the modern world, many institutions fall into a state that, where it to be detected in an individual, would be diagnosed as manic-depression!

Chaos theory tells us that while in some cases it is perfectly possible to control a system, in others a system may resist our attempts to redirect it. We turn the steering wheel and the system swerves and changes direction as expected, but then it settles back on exactly the same track as before. We apply yet more force on the wheel; the system swerves yet returns and defies our attempts at control. But in yet other situations even the slightest touch to the steering wheel may result in the system moving in some totally new and totally unpredictable direction.

The will to power

And so we have to come to terms with our traditional desire to be controllers of the world around us. The theoretical physicist, Wolfgang Pauli, argued that science had become obsessed with "the will to power", with a desire to dominate the natural world and force it to serve our own ends. This notion goes back to Francis Bacon who claimed that "knowledge is power" and suggested that nature should be placed on the rack and tormented in order that she would reveal her secrets.

There is a long tradition of our desire to dominate the natural world, to obtain all her secrets, to find "the ultimate theory", to live with certainty and to exercise absolute control. Yet, as I pointed out above, in the second half of the twentieth century science encountered hubris. It realized its own limitations and is now trying to teach us that these limitations apply to human society and organizations in general. It asks us to learn to live in harmony with nature rather than seeking to control her; to enter into dialogue with nature rather than attempting to shout her down; to combine our own intelligence and sensitivity with the innate intelligence and sensitivity of the natural world; to learn to live as partners rather than master and slave. But have we, our politicians and our organizations, really taken that lesson to heart?

Feedback

Chaos theory is trying to teach us these lessons, so let us now look at some of the insights it has brought with it. And, for the more technically inclined, I should add that the name "chaos theory" is a convenient blanket term for a range of approaches that involve nonlinear systems. In general the sort of systems we shall be exploring, both social and natural, are rich in what are called "feedback loops". Feedback occurs when one part of a system communicates its particular state of being to another. The thermostat in your house is an example of negative feedback. It is probably set at around 20°C or 70°F. In the winter, when the temperature in the room drops below these settings the thermostat detects this drop and sends an electrical signal that switches on the furnace. The room starts to heat up and when it reaches the required temperature the thermostat sends another signal, switching off the furnace. Hence negative feedback operates to stabilize a system. Something similar happens in the marketplace where negative feedback tends to stabilize the sales of a well-known product.

Positive feedback also involves a loop around the system, but here the effect is to destabilize the system. This occurs when a microphone is placed too close to a loudspeaker. A random sound is picked up by the microphone. It passes through the amplifier and is emitted by the loudspeaker, where it is picked up by the microphone, amplified and emitted yet again. After a few cycles a disturbingly loud, high-pitched sound can be heard.

Positive feedback can also operate when a brand new product appears on the market and may suddenly "take off". The paradigm example often given is of VHS and Betamax, two ways of making video recordings and playing videos. Engineers tended to favour Betamax as being superior, however it is nowhere to be seen today. The reason is that while the two competed for the same market, at some point VHS gained a very slight advantage. And this meant that people would be a little more likely to see a VHS player in a friend's house, and be able to borrow his or her VHS tapes. So why not choose to buy a VHS player and mention this to other friends? And so information loops around the system via positive feedback to constantly amplify VHS's position in the marketplace. As we shall see, positive and negative feedback are going to play key roles in the operation of those natural and human systems described by chaos theory.

Self-organization

London is one of the world's great cities. Not only is it an important centre for banking and trade but it also boasts the world's most active theatre districts and some of the world's greatest art collections. But no one designated that London be such a magnificent capital. No one took a map of Britain and marked a cross saying, "That's where we'll build the capital". London simply evolved and organized itself. Like Topsy in *Uncle Tom's Cabin*, London simply "growed". What's more, it wasn't just a village that grew into a town, and then grew into a city. The Romans had founded a settlement on the north bank of the Thames where it could be crossed by a bridge. This developed into "the City", a centre for trade and banking. Across the river was another settlement, the borough of Southwark with its hospitals and monasteries. In Elizabethan times this area then became renowned for its theatres (including Shakespeare's Globe), bear pits and brothels. Then, a mile upstream, the Abbey of Westminster had been built on what was an island in a marshy plain. Later it was to boast a royal palace and the centre of government. And so, unlike many other cities that are, at least, part planned, London simply evolved as each of these centres grew and began to swallow up other outlying villages. No one planned London, and to this day areas such as Bloomsbury, Hampstead, Blackheath and Greenwich retain a distinct identity as towns or villages within a major metropolis.

London is a wonderful example of what is termed "self-organization". It simply grew and organized itself as people, trade and money flowed through the city. Indeed it is generally true that when matter, or energy, or money, or information flows through a system, that system will begin to organize itself spontaneously. It will develop a physical structure, a pattern of behavior and a distinct identity, but without anyone having imposed this from outside.

Self-organization can also occur with traffic flows. Drive on a freeway in mid morning or late evening, and you can choose your own speed and proceed in an uninterrupted way without having to give much attention to other drivers. But during rush hours, traffic becomes heavier, everyone is more or less going at the same speed and are all locked together into one self-organized pattern.

A remarkable example of spontaneous organization is given by the slime mold in a wood or forest, which spends most of its life as a single-cell amoeba. But when the area in which individual slime molds reside becomes deprived of food, a chemical signal is sent out and the individual cells come together to form a cohesive whole, a slug-like entity which now begins to crawl along the forest floor. At some point the organism develops a stalk. Spores are ejected from the head of this stalk, which blow away until they fall to a new region of the forest floor and take life as new individual slime molds.

It is even possible to think of the human body as a form of self-organization, for it contains sub-units, such as the liver, kidneys, lungs and blood supply, which all work in harmony together, the whole being maintained in a state of homeostasis, so that any deviations from the norm—changes in temperature, levels of carbon dioxide in the blood, etc—are automatically corrected. Likewise, the flocking of birds and societies of bees and termites exhibit self-organization, as does the marketplace itself.

The food supply to New York City, and indeed to other of the world's major cities, is another case in point. There is no central bureaucracy that determines how the various components of the kitchen are to be shipped into the city, or how they are then to be distributed to supermarkets and corner stores. The whole thing emerged spontaneously; so that you can walk down a street in New York, buy an apple, a can of beans, a bagel, or a cup of coffee. No single individual or policy group organized this. It simply organized itself.

A more modern example is that of the Internet and the World Wide Web. Admittedly it had its origins in such things as ARPANET, when the US Department of Defence wanted to create a communications network that would survive in the case of nuclear attack, also NSFnet used by academic researchers, and a documentation project at the CERN nuclear research council in Switzerland. But having been given this kick-start, the Internet itself expanded way beyond anyone's expectations to around one billion users today. No one determined the structure and no one set out rules and regulations. (However, it should be added that the Internet has also spawned spam, hackers, fraud, pedophile rings and identity theft and there is a strong argument to be made that it should not continue to function in a totally unregulated fashion.)

Finally let me throw in one more, rather bizarre, example and this comes from Marvin Minsky, one of the fathers of the Artificial Intelligence movement. Minsky suggests that there is no central CEO in our brains, no overarching "I" who controls what we think, say or do. Rather, the brain is a collection of individual "actors", each with the capacity of operating independently.[5] However, as we develop from infancy, these individual units begin to cooperate and self-organize to form higher levels and eventually a "society of mind"—one capable of performing highly sophisticated tasks. Minsky also argues that human society has evolved a series of tactics that help the developing brain to self-organize. These include music and humour. Music teaches the brain to harmonize and coordinate. Likewise jokes are often based on upsetting our assumptions about the way the world, or society behaves. In other words, they alert us to rules, and to exceptions to rules, which is exactly the way a child learns.

Children make mistakes in grammar as they learn to speak. That is because they intuit a rule and assume that it applies in all cases. For example, we make the past participle of *sing* into *sung*, or *ring* into *rung* and so the child assumes that the past of *bring* must be *brung*. Likewise as we self-organize our knowledge we discover a rule, then the exception to that rule and then, at a higher level, possible exceptions to that exception.

One could continue with examples of a wide variety of self-organized systems, all of which will be found to have rich interwoven feedback loops. The major point is that in these cases no government, no policy group, and no external lawgiver created them. Rather, they emerged spontaneously and developed their own structures, their own rules, and their own codes of behavior. What is more, they like to continue to do what they have been doing in the past. If we don't happen to like what the system is doing, we may try to change its pattern of behavior. It is at this point that we discover that the system resists our attempts. If we push it, it may push back on us. Or maybe we push it and it changes direction for a moment, but a little later it is back again doing what it has always been doing.

Take, for example, a lake in which pike and trout have coexisted for decades. If someone attempts to stock the lake with many more trout, the pike will have a more abundant food supply and so their numbers will increase. But with more predators around, the number of trout will begin to fall and then, starved of food, the pike population itself will drop. With fewer pike the trout population rebounds. In this way the numbers of trout and pike slowly oscillate around their equilibrium values and no one species gets to dominate the environment. These examples are repeated again and again within ecosystems, and even in a stable marketplace.

Like living systems, self-organized systems stabilize and even heal themselves. However, the situation may be different when something totally new enters an already well-established and stable self-organized system. Take the case of Thomas Austin from England who enjoyed a regular weekend's rabbit shooting in his home countryside. When he moved to Australia he wished to continue with his hobby and so in 1859 he asked his nephew to send him 24 rabbits, along with some other species such as partridges. For hundreds of thousands of years Australia had been a continent cut off from the rest of the world and had established its own self-organized equilibrium of flora and fauna. But when it came to rabbits, there were no natural predators around, and so the population increased rapidly. Within ten years the original 24 had multiplied to the extent that two million rabbits could be trapped and shot annually without having a noticeable effect on the population. As a result of the introduction of a foreign species, (along with European methods of farming and land clearing) one eighth of Australia's mammal species became extinct. In addition, by eating plants whose roots bound the earth, rabbits also produced serious soil erosion. In the end Australia introduced the Myxoma virus, which caused an epidemic of Myxomatosis and helped to wipe out a significant proportion of the rabbit population.[6]

Of even greater significance was the introduction of European diseases into North America. While there had been occasional outbreaks of epidemics such as plague, Black Death and, the deadly strain of influenza of 1918-1919, Europeans had more or less developed a natural immunity to many diseases, an immunity not possessed by the original inhabitants of North America. European diseases were probably first carried by animals that escaped from ships fishing off the west coast of North America, as well as those brought by the first settlers. As these animals migrated into the hinterland, microorganisms and viruses were spread to the human population. While estimates vary, some put the death rate of the indigenous people of North America as high as 90 percent.[7] This far exceeds the death rate from the Black Death, which in various parts of Europe wiped out between one eighth and one third of the population. (It should be added that in some cases extinction of the native population was intentional, as when blankets contaminated with smallpox were given to them. An exchange of letters between General Amherst—commander of the British Forces during the French and Indian wars of 1754-1763—and Colonel Bouquet suggests that this was their intention.)[8]

The lesson to be learned from this section is that, yes, it may be quite difficult to change the behavior of a self-organized system and push it in a direction we may prefer. On the other hand we must always be careful when we make an intervention from outside, for introducing something new into such a system may cause total disruption.

When systems fail

We have seen that one thing that can disrupt a self-organized system is the introduction of something totally new. Now let us see what could happen if feedback loops become compromised? Take the city of Liverpool as an example.[9] It was once one of England's most prosperous cities. As a seaport, it was a key centre for goods being shipped to and from the United States and Canada. Earlier it had been the hub for the great emigrations from Ireland and Europe to the New World (particularly after the Great Potato Famine in Ireland).

Liverpool built its first docks in the 18th century when it traded with the Americas and West Indies. Then, in 1830, the Liverpool and Manchester railway was opened to allow goods to be shipped for export from Liverpool, arriving from all of Britain's major manufacturing centres. (Ironically it was also the scene of the first railway accident! On the day of the opening, William Huskisson, the Member of Parliament for Liverpool, started to cross the track to speak to the Duke of Wellington when he was hit by Stephenson's *Rocket* and died later that day. The *Rocket* had a speed of around 10 miles per hour.)

Liverpool's economy meant hiring crew to man the ships, and employing dockers (longshoremen) to handle cargo. A harbour master and his staff, as well as people to maintain the dockyards, were also required. And, in the days before computers, an army of clerks was needed to do the necessary paperwork in shipping offices and marine insurance offices. Across the river, the city of Birkenhead became a centre for shipbuilding. Add to this all the service industries, such as transport (buses, trucks and the docklands railway), road maintenance, postal service, restaurants, solicitors, schools, doctors, hospitals, corner stores, clothing stores, marine suppliers, and it was pretty clear that most of the economy of an entire city rested on one thing—shipping. (There were also smaller industries in and around Liverpool such as chemical plants and Hartley's jam factory.)

A city such as Liverpool functioned because money was constantly flowing through the entire system. Manufacturers paid shipping companies to transport their products. Shipping companies hired dockers to move these goods. Dockers needed to get to work early each morning. The bus driver, in the best Liverpool tradition, gave his weekly wage packet to his wife to buy food for the table. The corner shop bought its jam from Hartley's. Hartley's employed workers to make the jam and so on. So money and goods were constantly circulating through the city in a series of feedback loops. Liverpool was a self-organized system and self-organized systems require a healthy nesting of feedback loops in order to survive, as well as a flow-through of goods, energy and/or money. A city, a region and an economy are all healthy when they support a diversity of activities linked together by feedback loops in which the output of one activity becomes the input for another.

And so the city grew and prospered and would have continued in this way if something new hadn't happened. What occurred was the introduction of container transport. This meant larger ships, which, in turn, required bigger container docks. Liverpool was not quick enough in building these container docks and so the majority of goods now left from the Rotterdam docks in Holland, or by air. No longer were great sums of money flowing into Liverpool and being passed, as money, goods and work, through the city's feedback loops. Prosperity declined and unemployment rose. In essence the city could not support the inner web of complexity that allowed it to survive. Feedback was the very thing that had allowed the city to grow and prosper. In London feedback continued to operate, but in Liverpool it was compromised. While it is true that the city has recovered to a certain degree and was Europe's Capital of Culture in 2008, for some time it remained one of the poorest areas in England. Its unemployment rate is still around 11 percent and its crime rate is double that of the national average.

Attractors and fractals

Self-organized systems develop their own laws and patterns of behavior that can be remarkably robust. Push the system and it may resist, or change for a time but then settle back to its original behavior. Chaos theorists therefore speak of such systems as being in the grip of "attractors" that determine their behavior. An attractor could be compared to a round bowl with a glass marble rotating inside. The marble goes round and round in the bowl repeating the same pattern. Here I should point out that the attractor is not something external to the system, imposed from outside. Rather the self-organizing system has evolved its own structure that can be conveniently pictured in terms of variously shaped attractors.

There are also more complex systems that are in the grip of what are called "strange attractors". Normal attractors have regular shapes such as a bowl or a donut. You can picture the behavior of the system as moving from one point on the bowl to the point right next to it, so its behavior is quite orderly and predictable. But a strange attractor has what is known as a fractal structure and to go any further in understanding this we need to know a little more about fractals.

You have probably seen posters with images of fractals—certainly you will have seen images associated with Benoit Mandelbrot's fractals. Fractals are shapes containing infinite detail. In the case of the Mandelbrot fractal, zoom in on one piece of detail and you will see it repeated at finer and finer scales. This is referred to as self-similarity.

Fractals not only describe complex systems in the natural world, such as coastlines, clouds, fractures in metals and so on, but they also apply to human situations. It is often said that an entire fairy tale is contained, implicitly, within its opening lines. Why should this be? Well fairy stories deal in archetypical situations—a hero's journey, a young woman's awakening, a wicked stepmother, a riddle to be answered. Jungians would say that while the actual manifestation of an archetype, as a particular image, story or human behavior, can be highly varied, the underlying pattern of a particular archetype is always the same. These archetypes are attractors for images, stories and human behaviors and what is more, they are fractal attractors—they are strange attractors. And we know that fractals exhibit self-similarity at ever decreasing scales. So while the details of a particular fairy story that begins—"There was once a poor boy, the youngest of three brothers"—will vary from story to story, and is therefore to a degree unpredictable from sentence to sentence, we do know that at some point this boy is going to go on a journey, meet some adversary, triumph in some task and find his reward in marrying a princess. So fairy stories exhibit fractal self-similarity. Likewise some therapists say that the whole issue of a patient's life, and the pattern of the therapy, are contained within the first interview or even in the first few sentences that a new patient utters.

While self-organized systems in the grip of a normal attractor have strict repetitive behavior, those in the grip of a strange attractor will be unpredictable from moment to moment. For a regular attractor, the system moves from one point on the attractor's surface to one nearby and so produces a smooth change of behavior. However, with a fractal attractor things are much more complicated, and behavior will jump in an unpredictable way. Nevertheless, while we don't know the system's behavior from moment to moment (just as we don't know exactly what the next sentence will be in a new fairy tale), we may also be able to detect overall trends and patterns. The fluctuations of the stock market are a case in point. While we cannot predict the exact value of a particular stock from hour to hour we will note a general trend. We will also detect fractal self-similarity in that the fluctuations over a year look similar to those over a week, or a day, or an hour.

In the previous section we learned that some systems develop their own self-organization and can be remarkably stable in their repetitive behavior, provided we do not introduce something radically new from outside. In this section we learned of different sorts of attractors, called strange attractors, which give rise to systems that may be totally unpredictable from moment to moment, yet may have some overall self-similar pattern within their behavior.

The butterfly effect

On December 1, 1955 an African-American woman boarded a bus in Montgomery, Alabama and sat in the first row of the "colored" seating. As the journey continued, several white people boarded the bus until the white section was filled and three passengers were standing. Under the bylaws of the city, the driver had the power to assign seating and so he requested passengers in the first colored row to give up their seats. All did, except for one black woman, Rosa Louise Parks.[10] She was arrested and her lawyers suggested that she should use the case as a challenge to the city's segregation policy. The end result, as everyone knows, was the birth of the Civil Rights Movement and the end of segregation in the South. The small action on the part of one individual produced a radical social change in an entire nation.

This case is often quoted as an example of "the butterfly effect"— that the flapping of a butterfly's wings in one place can cause a major change in weather the other side of the world. But in order to understand this butterfly effect we should look more closely at the Rosa Parks case. To begin with it had all been done before, but to no real effect. For example, in 1944 the athlete Jackie Robinson had refused to move. Ten years later, 15-year old Claudette Colvin was handcuffed and forcibly removed for the same violation. So small actions do not always produce great results. What is required is that these actions occur at a critical point in critical time and in exactly the right way.

What was different in the Rosa Parks case? Well, one of her lawyers was Clifford Durr who had previously worked in Washington defending those who had been accused of being fellow travellers or communists during the McCarthy era. (Amongst those he represented was the theoretical physicist, David Bohm). His passion, therefore, was for the defence of civil liberties, of which civil rights were a part. And there was another coincidence: Rosa Parks worked for the Durrs as a housekeeper and seamstress!

Parks's lawyers hit on the idea of a bus boycott and the Montgomery Improvement Association was formed. This group decided to elect as their president a young, and relatively unknown, Baptist minister, Martin Luther King, Jr. And so this particular butterfly was created through the fortuitous intersection of several significant people. The rest is history. The vast majority of Montgomery's 40,000 black commuters boycotted the city's buses for 382 days and the Civil Rights Movement was born. There was yet another factor. White families employed members of the Black community as maids, cooks, cleaners, gardeners and so on. But now they were refusing to take the bus. This meant that someone had to drive over to pick up their employees, and so members of the white community were applying political pressure to bring the boycott to an end. The success of the Montgomery incident also inspired a boycott in Alexandria, South Africa and led to a radicalization of that country under the African National Congress.

The lesson of the butterfly effect is that small effects do not necessarily produce big changes, but with exactly the right conditions, and within the right context, a tiny action can have an enormously transforming effect. That is one of the things we would hope to achieve with Gentle Action. If Claire and Gordon Shippey had not visited Pari they would never have transformed an area of their hometown. And as we will see later in this book, if certain other conditions had not already been in place in Middlesbrough, Gordon's action of knocking on doors may have produced little effect.

The term "butterfly effect" was in fact coined by Edward Lorenz, a meteorologist. In the early 1960s he was running computerized equations used to predict weather conditions. After having run one particular sequence, he decided to replicate it. Lorenz reentered the number from his printout and left the program to run. When he came to check the results he discovered that they were radically different from his first outcome. What had happened was that rather than entering the precise figure 0.506127 he had used a rounded-off figure of 0.506. At the time he had assumed that a small error in the initial conditions would produce a small change in the final outcome. But Lorenz's computer program was using what is called iteration. That is, the output from one calculation becomes the input for the next. In the real world this is represented by a feedback loop—that is, information flows round and round a system. So that, when positive feedback is involved, the tiniest change in initial conditions rapidly becomes amplified as it circulates around the system. In December 1972 at a meeting of the American Association for the Advancement of Science in Washington Lorenz announced the famous butterfly effect with his talk, "Predictability: Does the flap of a butterfly's wings in Brazil set off a tornado in Texas?"

When Claudette Colvin refused to move to the back of the bus her action did not iterate around the system and amplify. But Rosa Parks had lawyers who wanted to make her arrest into a test case, and so her action began to iterate around the African-American community. It was amplified by the Montgomery Improvement Association and by a charismatic leader, Martin Luther King. Finally it blossomed into a major social nonviolent action—a bus boycott. In turn, this boycott gave rise to the civil rights movement both in the United States and as an opposition to apartheid in South Africa. Social change was created out of a tiny action but it was an action performed in just the right conditions to cause a social tornado.

Butterfly cookies

I am grateful to Melissa Cassas for the following example of her own personal experience of the butterfly effect. She sent it to me while she was taking an Internet-based course I was teaching at the California Institute of Integral Studies and we happened to be discussing the butterfly effect and the case of Rosa Parks.

In 1995 Melissa was baking chocolate chip cookies according to a particular recipe, but made mistakes with some of the measurements. Rather than being a disaster, the result was an original and very tasty cookie, which she called "Melissa's Cookies". Her friends kept asking for samples and, having worked in the baking industry, she wondered if she should turn her cookies into a small business. In fact she started to research the market, but for some reason the time just didn't seem right to her.

Six years later she enrolled in a Masters program at John F. Kennedy University, which involved a course on "starting your own business". Again the idea of going commercial with her cookies came up and she went so far as to develop a brand name and a logo, but the time and the conditions again did not seem appropriate and so she embarked on creating a different sort of business.

Over the next years requests kept pouring in for her cookies, which she gave out for free. At the same time she was becoming frustrated and dissatisfied with her own business. Why not go for the cookies? But, in her own words, it was "wrong time, wrong conditions". Then in November 2006, she baked cookies for a friend and a week later the woman's husband asked if he could place an order. "In that split second I knew the time was *now* to begin the business." Melissa wrote, "I told him I would get back to him with a price list, and in that moment 'Ms. M's Cookies' was officially launched."

Within two weeks the business was up and running, with a website www.msmcookies.com and international sales. As Melissa says "It was truly a living example of the butterfly effect. From that one small conversation...feedback loops of massive proportion have moved me into a full-blown cookie business. What made that conversation with my colleague on November 27 any different from hundreds of other comments...? I was in a different place and time in my life, and it was time to act on my idea...I had learned how to listen to the signals of force that sometimes come into play. It is a very different experience riding a wave that has just presented itself, versus trying to create a wave to ride."

Missing information

As we have seen, a system in the grip of a normal attractor has predictable behavior, while one in the grip of a strange attractor behaves in a moment-to-moment, unpredictable way. A strange attractor has endless detail and therefore, while a self-organized system obeying a strange attractor may exhibit trends and patterns, its moment-to-moment behavior cannot be exactly predicted. In other words, we cannot exhaustively describe such a system. Likewise, with the "butterfly effect" a tiny change can make a radical difference to a system. This means that the system has reached what is called a bifurcation point and is infinitely sensitive to the context around it. Chaos theorists would say that it is extremely sensitive to its initial conditions—that is, to the conditions that define its state of being.

In other words, there will be some systems for which we simply cannot gather sufficient information to provide an exhaustive description, or to be able to predict their future behavior with certainty. This is the issue of "missing information". Even with the help of the world's largest computers there will be some systems we can never fully describe and some forms of behavior we can never fully predict.

Solitons

Melissa Cassas found a wave on which to ride, so maybe it is now time to learn about another remarkable type of wave, which may bear, some relationship to the one Melissa discovered. Throw a rock into still water and you create a splash that begins to travel outwards and soon dissipates. The reason is not difficult to see if we look at another type of disturbance— sound. It is easy to recognize when a violin, trumpet or saxophone is playing. Each instrument has a very characteristic sound. The reason is that, in addition to the fundamental note—middle C, say—being played, there are also a whole series of overtones—vibrations of higher and higher frequency. Each musical instrument has a different mixture of overtones that give it its characteristic sound. The case of a disturbance in water is exactly analogous. That splash is made up of a series of wavelets each with a different wavelength. As it turns out, the speed at which a wavelet travels in water depends upon its wavelength. So when the splash begins to move outward the shorter wavelengths move on ahead and the slower ones lag behind. Pretty soon all the different wavelengths have separated and the effects of the splash can no longer be seen.

But this is not always the case. In 1834 a Scottish engineer, John Scott Russell, was riding his horse along the banks of the Union Canal near Edinburgh when he saw a boat that was being drawn by a pair of horses suddenly stop. The wave that had been created at the bow of the boat continued to move along the canal without dissipating. Russell followed this wave for one or two miles, moving at a constant speed of eight or nine miles per hour, until he lost it "in the windings of the channel". This wave puzzled Russell for the rest of his life and he set out to find other examples.[11] Had he lived in South America he would have known that the "bore" of the Amazon River can be as high as 25 feet and will travel for over 500 miles without breaking apart.

Since wavelets of different wavelengths travel at different speeds how was it possible for Russell's wave to travel for two miles? The reason is that non-linear effects were operating towards the bottom of the canal. These had the effect of coupling all the different wavelets together. In many different sorts of systems, and under certain critical conditions, it is possible for the various components of a wave to couple together so that something called a soliton is born; a wave that will persist intact for long periods. Solitons can also occur in the atmosphere. In 1951 a mass of cold air around 100 miles long travelled across Kansas at a speed of 12 mph for several hundred miles. The famous Red Spot on Jupiter is also a soliton, as are the electrical impulses that travel along nerve pathways. In fact it turns out that solitons occur in many different systems when individual components (wavelets) bond together to form a collective. And so, in a certain way, solitons are also an important form of organization within nonlinear systems, one in which effects produced in one region will propagate into another. I will return to the example of a soliton when we look at Gentle Action in more detail.

Intermittency: Order and chaos

Chaos theory deals in a very wide range of systems; from some that are totally repetitive and difficult to change, to systems with overall trends of behavior but which are unpredictable from moment to moment; from systems in which the tiniest puff of wind will produce a massive butterfly effect, to systems which are totally chaotic.

Now let us look at some interesting systems that combine both order and chaos. Carnival, the word literally means "Go away meat", is the Christian festival held before Lent. Some of the best known carnivals are associated with the towns of Rio de Janeiro and Venice. It is a time of feasting and drinking, for partying and practical jokes, for the dissolution of social divisions and sexual prohibitions. To a puritanical mind it may look like the total breakdown of social order. But are things that clear cut? Is what appears to us as social chaos the total lack of any order, or an order of a highly subtle degree?

Let us look at this question by way of a robot machine designed to turn out parts. Suppose you feed instructions into the machine by way of digital data. What is the simplest instruction you can give the machine? Answer: a single number. With a single number the machine can only turn out a sphere—the radius of the sphere being that particular number. Now suppose you progressively add in more numbers within the list of instructions. The machine may turn out a cube, then an irregular cube and so on, progressively producing shapes of greater and greater complexity. With the simpler shapes it is possible to look at them from one side and guess what the other side will look like. But as the quantity of numbers in the instructions increase, the shapes become filled with more and more baroque detail so that, given information about one region of the shape, it is increasingly difficult to predict how another region will look. Finally with an infinite amount of information being fed to the robot we have a shape, which, to all intents and purposes, is random and chaotic.

So, rather than saying that chaos is the breakdown of all order, it may be better to say that chaos is an order of infinitely high degree, a pattern produced by an infinite amount of information or input.

Now back to the *carnevale* of Venice. Is it really a total breakdown of social order? No. The tradition of the *carnevale* is based on subtle and mutually understood rules. To begin with everyone is masked: They are able to preserve their anonymity. Whatever they do that night will not be held against them in the future—by a spouse or social superior. There is a social contract to anonymity, everyone agrees to the temporary suspension of certain structures. (Note that at a time when homosexual acts were punishable by death, the authorities in Venice ruled that a masked male homosexual had the legal status of a masked woman and so no offence was committed.)

It could be argued that some societies survive by means of alternating periods of simple order, when rather rigid sets of rules apply, and periods of complex and subtle order. For much of the year a well-defined social order reigns, then at *carnevale* that order breaks down in favour of a more subtle order. At the start of Lent that subtle order breaks down into a more rigid order. Likewise Munich celebrates its famous Oktoberfest.

This phenomenon of alternation between order and "chaos" is also well known in a variety of physical systems and is technically termed intermittency. Intermittency can occur in certain types of electronic amplifiers when periods of regular activity are followed by bursts of noise. They also occur in the cycles of activity of the sun, including the appearance of sunspots, as well as in turbulent water, and in the "wobble" in the earth's rotation. This interweaving of simple and complex orders can take place when networks of computers and parallel processors are coupled together. It is as if complex orders are always lurking within what appear to be regular and well behaved systems. Again it is this combination of nested feedback loops that can move us between different domains of order. So when we consider the nature of organizations, economies and societies we must always keep in mind that rules and orders can be of different degrees, and that one order may at times segue into another.

The final lesson of this chapter is that the orderly Newtonian clockwork world represents only a very small section of the vast richness of natural and social systems that surround us. For several centuries science sought certainty and closure within its theories. One of the great lessons of the twentieth century was taught to us by chaos theory—that there is a limitation to what we can know, to how much we can predict, and the degree to which we can bend situations to our own will. We have learned that so many systems and forms of organization are far more complicated, or sensitive, than we ever supposed and that we must learn to dance with nature rather then seek to turn it into our slave.

✂ Reflections on Chapter 2

1. How do you feel when there is uncertainty in your life or when you face situations in which you lack full information? Does it make you uncomfortable, or is there a certain exhilaration in not fully knowing what is going to happen next? And what do you think of when you hear the world "chaos"? How does that make you think and feel?

2. Under which situations do you feel it important to remain in control, and in which cases can you relax your control?

3. What about working with groups? What role should a leader have? Think of those leaders in history, or at your work, or in your own community who lead by marching ahead of everyone else, and of those who lead though facilitation.

4. This chapter also explored power and the desire to dominate nature. Do you know individuals who love to exercise such power? If so, what effects do they have on the people around them and the organizations in which they work?

5. Describe your own experiences of self-organization? Have you been a member of a group or team that suddenly began to work in harmony together without any one person appearing to have set an agenda? If so, can you figure out how this happened? And what about cases in which an existing group fell apart into sub groups, or when individuals opted out? What were the causes?

6. Do you have any examples of the butterfly effect in your own life, community or organization? If so why not share them with the rest of us via www.gentleaction.org.

Notes

1. Rachel Carson, *Silent Spring* (New York: Houghton Mifflin, 1962).

2. E. F. Schumacher, *Small is Beautiful* (New York: Harper Perennial, 1973).

3. An overview of chaos theory can be found in John Briggs and F. David Peat, *Turbulent Mirror*, (New York: Harper & Row, 1989) and in *Seven Life Lessons of Chaos* (New York: Harper Collins, 1999) by the same authors.

4. James Lovelock, *The Revenge of Gaia* (Cambridge, MA: Perseus, 2007).

5. Marvin Minsky's ideas can be found in, *Society of Mind* (New York: Simon & Schuster, 1988).

6. For Thomas Austin and the release of rabbits see, for example, http://www.animalcontrol.com.au/rabbit.htm.

7. See, for example, F. David Peat, *Blackfoot Physics* (Grand Rapids, MI: Phanes Press, 2002).

8. For the letters between Amherst and Bouquet see, for example, http://www.nativeweb.org/pages/legal/amherst/lord_jeff.html.

9. The example of Liverpool comes from my own personal experience. See, for example, http://en.wikipedia.org/wiki/Liverpool.

10. See, for example, her obituary in the *New York Times* for October 25, 2005. Her biography can also be found at www.rosaparks.org also Rosa Parks and Jim Haskins, *Rosa Parks: My Story*, (New York: Puffin, 1999).

11. See note 4.

Chapter 3.
Controlling complexity

As we saw in the previous chapter, unlike mechanical systems, such as cars and trains, natural and social systems can be enormously complex and subtle, and they can exhibit markedly different forms of behavior in different regions or contexts. Some natural systems are relatively simple, well behaved and predictable, others are enormously complex and beyond our ability to fully describe or control. What is more, some systems can also shift behavior between these two extremes in unexpected ways. A system may move along in a fairly predicable way as we interact with it, until it has a feeling of familiarity about it. We lean on the system and it leans back on us then, after some time, while we are leaning on it, it suddenly shoves back at us, or it steps out of the way and allows us to fall flat on our face. At times we may think we know where we are going and are lulled into not giving full attention to what is happening until it is too late. The lesson we must learn is that when we make an intervention in a system we may feel that everything is going smoothly, but if we don't know the full and complex details of how that system operates, then down the line we could run into trouble. Let me give some examples of what can happen when obvious and simple solutions are applied to systems that are more complex than we first anticipated; or in which individuals or organizations never really bothered to understand the systems or societies they were dealing with.

Freon and lead

Freon is the generic name for a number of chlorofluorocarbon gases that were used in refrigerators and aerosols. The gases are colorless, odorless, nonflammable and noncorrosive. They seemed ideal for the job. They were totally harmless to humans, and ran no risk of contaminating food, or causing a fire if they happened to leak. But what no one anticipated was that, in the upper atmosphere, sunlight breaks down the Freon molecules to release chlorine, which then reacts with ozone. The result is that Freon, leaking from refrigerators and released from aerosols, caused a hole to develop in the ozone layer over the north and south poles. This is where the human hazard begins, for ozone acts to filter out the harmful ultraviolet rays that can cause skin cancer. As a result of the use of Freon, skin cancers are now on the increase worldwide but particularly in such countries as Chile and Australia. Here another ironic twist can be added. Because of the fear of skin cancer some people have begun to use strong sun blocks. As a consequence, vitamin D deficiency is on the rise! (The body uses sunlight in the production of vitamin D.)

Another unpredictable factor was the use of lead in gasoline to increase the efficiency of automobile engines. This began in the 1920s, a period when there were far fewer automobiles on the road. It looked like an ideal solution until, by the 1970s, people became worried about air pollution in cities. Not only was there a haze from car exhausts but an increase of lead in the environment. Scientists became concerned about the prolonged exposure of children to this lead, particularly the action it had on the nervous system. The result was the banning of lead additives, but not before damage had been already been done to the brains of inner-city children.[1]

The Green Revolution

What could be nobler than relieving starvation and feeding the world? In 1943 four million people died of famine in eastern India. The causes of the famine were complex; it was not so much a question of floods or a major crop failure, but that the war in Europe had made the issue of food supply of low priority to the British rulers in India. Therefore when India became independent it was determined to tackle the issue of food and agriculture, and so the Green Revolution was born.[2]

The origins of this revolution began in 1945 when, with the help of the Rockefeller foundation, a project was initiated to increase yields of wheat in Mexico. The endeavour was under the supervision of Norman Borlaug who was later awarded the Nobel Peace Prize for his work. The approach appeared highly successful, since within twelve years Mexico went to a position of self-sufficiency from initially having to import half its wheat. This program was then applied in India and Pakistan. Finally the Green Revolution became a highly desired global transformation of agriculture and food supply. But, as we shall see, by imposing a plan from outside and without taking into account all the subtle and complex conditions of particular human societies, it also produced some undesirable side effects.

The program involved a two-pronged approach. The first was to replace indigenous crops by hybrid strains of wheat and rice known to produce high yields. The second prong was to transform existing agricultural practice. Thus, the hybrids were designed to be harvested mechanically and to respond well to chemical fertilizers. In addition, this intensive agriculture required the use of pesticides and herbicides. Finally, with improved irrigation, it was possible to produce two crops per year in some areas instead of one.

The result was a substantial improvement in the production of wheat and rice in many parts of the world. In addition, farming became less labour intensive. Taken at face value the Green Revolution would appear to be a positive good for humanity. On the other hand, it has also come under increasing criticism. Clearly some of this could have been predicted from the onset. Focusing on single hybrids clearly reduces biodiversity. Left to herself nature exploits diversity. If one variety of a plant is subject to disease, insect attack and so on, another will soon fill the gap. Lack of diversity was the cause of the Irish Potato Famine. The British rulers focused on potatoes as a major source of food for the Irish population—eventually that crop was subject to a fungus that wiped out the potatoes and resulted in the death from starvation of 1.1 million of the Irish people.[3]

In addition, a variety of doubts have been expressed about the Green Revolution such as populations experiencing lower nutritional value, since they are increasingly dependent on a one-food source. Likewise, the toxicity of the pesticides used also eliminated fish from paddy fields (another source of food) and killed indigenous plants that provided vegetables for the local people, as well as being toxic to farmers who do not always take adequate protection.

There is yet another side to this, the total disruption of a social structure when the labour-intensive farming of a variety of indigenous crops in developing nations is transferred into the mechanized farming of monocultures. What is more, countries that adopted the Green Revolution discovered that they had become locked into a relationship with the multinationals that supply the seeds, fertilizers, pesticides, herbicides and ripeners. What appeared at first sight to have been a gift from the First World to the Third ended up being a debt that had to be paid by these same developing nations. Moreover, in many cases farmers had to enter into a contract stating that they would no longer plant any of their own indigenous crops or collect and store seeds.

Donated clothing

Donated clothing is the lifeblood of many charity organizations and while around 20 percent of this clothing is sold in charity shops, the rest is shipped abroad. This seems like a positive good—to supply secondhand clothing to the Third World. Not so. In 1991 Zambia boasted 140 textile manufacturers. By 2002 there were only eight. The cause? A glut of cheap secondhand clothing that has killed Zambia's clothing manufacturing base.[4]

Tower blocks

Housing relates directly to the structuring of human society. I well recall a visit to our village in Tuscany by the architect, Christopher Alexander. He told me that architecture and urban planning actually affects the consciousness of the people living in a town or city. Take our own village of Pari, for example, which is very much a protecting environment. I can recall a woman who had Alzheimer's disease and who would wander around the village—yet somehow the arrangement of the village streets contained her and she never wandered away; going down the hill and out of the village, for example. The village also has spaces where people can naturally congregate and talk, and a piazza where most of the village meets in the evening. This is architecture at its best, for the village has evolved from century to century as a home for a community.

But what happens when architecture does not evolve in a natural way? Take, for example, the way tower blocks (highrise apartment blocks) were employed in Britain. Following World War II, the Labour government felt an urgent need to create new housing for people who were living in overcrowded conditions in poorer areas of cities. The centres of many cities had been bombed and, in others, people lived in Victorian-era houses with unsanitary conditions. The idea was to provide modern accommodation for large numbers of people and the solution was to build vertically, so that more families could be accommodated on a moderately sized piece of land—the solution became known as "tower blocks".

At first sight they seemed ideal—people from poorer areas could move into modern highrise apartments equipped with central heating, bathrooms and fitted kitchens, plus spectacular views of the city. In Greater London alone, some 2700 tower blocks were built from 1949 until the mid-1970s. The highest concentration of blocks was found in Glasgow.

But gradually enthusiasm for this form of housing began to wane. Admittedly people had previously been living in poor and overcrowded conditions, but at least they knew their neighbors, who would pop in to chat or borrow a cup of sugar. They could help each other with shopping and watch out as children played together in the street outside. In other words, there was a strong social fabric at work, one in which people looked out for each other's interest. People knew exactly what was happening in the streets around them, and in effect could do their own community policing. It was a society somewhat similar to that portrayed in the working-class British soap opera, *Coronation Street*—a far cry from the lifestyles of *Dallas* or *The Bold and the Beautiful.*

But now that a person lived many storeys above ground level, he or she could no longer communicate easily which those living several floors below. Moreover, it was difficult for small children to play together when they lived at different levels. And so the previously strong social fabric began to decay and, with time, the quality of the physical buildings also degraded. The inevitable result was that petty and sometimes serious crime (drug-dealing in stairwells, for example) began to rise and the buildings were increasingly vandalized. In this way a spiral was created in which an environment of crime and vandalization created yet more crime and vandalization—another example of a feedback loop.

During the 1980s several of the tower blocks were demolished. Then in the 1990s some were refurbished and became fashionable dwelling places for young professionals. The problem therefore did not so much lie in architectural design itself but in imposing a form of housing on a selected group of society—the close-knit street-based culture of the urban poor—without fully understanding or anticipating the consequences. After all, highrise apartment buildings were also built in North America and became agreeable homes for a different type of society—young singles, childless couples, retirees, etc.[5]

A bridge too far

Members of the Peace Corps working in Guatemala decided to build a bridge across a particular river but didn't listen when the local people told them it simply couldn't be done.[6] After all, they had so much superior technology at their backs compared to the locals. Their first step was to spend several months constructing a road so that they could bring in a large earth mover. With the earth mover finally in place, they then began to create a very large ramp on one side of the river. But then the rainy season began and the river changed its course to the point where it was now located a mile away. The result was that they were left with a useless ramp in the middle of the jungle. If they had bothered to listen to the local people they would have learned that it was not unusual for the river to change its course.

Nile perch

In the previous chapter we saw an example of what happens when something new is introduced into a stable self-organized system such as an ecosystem. A few rabbits introduced into Australia resulted in the extinction of a number of natural species. Another example, which has also had a devastating effect on a human population, comes from Africa. Lake Victoria is the world's second largest freshwater lake and is shared by Kenya, Tanzania and Uganda. Once its waters were clear and filled with a large variety of species, but today it is murky, choked with algae and dominated by one species—the Nile perch. It appears to be one of the worst, and probably irreversible, ecological disasters created by a human intervention that was based on initial good intentions.[7]

For many centuries the indigenous population had existed in harmony with the lake, taking much of its protein from fish. But after colonization by the British, the lakeside population began to grow and fishing techniques improved; but with over-fishing the catch sizes started to drop and some species even became extinct. Since fish were a major source of protein in the area, during the 1950s British officials decided to introduce new species into the lake. In this case people were not working in ignorance of possible consequences, for the proposal was opposed by scientists who feared that it might destroy the lake's natural ecosystem. Nevertheless, a fisheries officer was ordered to introduce, in a clandestine manner, a species known as Nile perch—a fish that grows to a large size and that had no natural predators in the lake. Additional quantities of Nile perch were also intentionally added in the early 1960s.

During the first decades it looked as if the scientists may have been wrong, for the Nile perch accounted for only a tiny percentage of the lake's fish, with smaller indigenous species known as cichlids making up 80 percent of Lake Victoria's biomass. Then, in 1980, scientists realized that a drastic change had occurred, with cichlids being reduced to only one percent of the biomass and the Nile perch accounting for 80 percent. In addition, with the absence of significant numbers of fish species that feed on detritus, organic materials in the lake began to decay and consumed oxygen in the process. As a result, some areas of the lake are so depleted of oxygen that they are uninhabitable—essentially "dead" areas. Some scientists have called the situation in Lake Victoria "the greatest vertebrate mass extinction in recorded history".

But it was not only the lake's ecology that was affected, but also the lives of the many communities that live near to the lake, and even as far away as Eastern Europe. For centuries men had fished the lake with small boats and small nets, and women boned the fish. But the Nile perch, which is now the dominant species, lives too far out in open water for the little fishing boats; in addition the traditional nets are too small to catch the fish which simply rip though the netting. As a consequence, the natural source of protein for the large number of people who live around the lake has almost dried up and once self-sufficient communities have been reduced to poverty.

However business people, from outside the area, saw a golden opportunity to introduce a new industry. They brought in large commercial fishing vessels, which sold their catch to foreign-owned processing plants that were built at the lakeside. Where once the local women had filleted the fish, this process was now done at factory level where the fish were filleted, frozen and exported to Europe and the Middle East as an expensive delicacy. The result was that the local men no longer had work, and the local women were reduced to processing fish waste discarded from the filleting plants. Ironically with the rise in the cost of fish, protein malnutrition increased in an area that exports 200,000 tons of fish annually. What is more, pollution in the lake, together with the dumping of raw sewage, has increased the incidence of typhoid, cholera and diarrhoea.

There are other costs. The amount of wood needed to dry the Nile perch has resulted in deforestation of some areas. In addition, the crew of the commercial fishing vessels generally come from other areas of Africa attracted by high wages. But they are single men and, as a result, prostitution has increased with the corresponding rise in Aids. The pilots of the cargo planes used to export the fish tend to come from Eastern Europe and also make use of the local prostitutes, which means taking the HIV virus back to their home countries. What is more, many of these pilots also have arrangements with arms dealers and import weapons and ammunition into Africa in the same planes used to export the fish.

For many business people and investors the Nile perch has become a boom industry, but for the lake itself and the lives of the local people it remains a major disaster. Unlike many of the other examples in this book, this particular incident was not created out of ignorance of the complexities of the system, for scientists had warned officials of the consequences. Maybe it was simply a case of the bureaucratic attitude that "we know better" and "we're doing it for their own good".

Buffalo grass

Before the Europeans came to North America the Great Plains were covered in hardy buffalo grass whose roots penetrate five feet into the soil.

When fires, set off by lightning strikes, would sweep across the Plains, the roots remained protected by the soil and the plants appeared to grow even better after being burned. Moreover the deep roots bound the soil to prevent erosion. But as the North American population increased, wheat with its much shorter root system, replaced the buffalo grass.[8] As a result, soil in the Great Plains is being seriously eroded, primarily by winds, but also from rain. Eventually one of the most fertile areas of the United States and Canada will be reduced to a dust bowl.

Eleven-plus and trust in science

Beginning in 1944 with the Butler Education Act, the British adopted an examination system taken by children at the age of eleven in order to determine which type of secondary school they would attend. The "eleven-plus" examination tested basic skills in mathematics and English with an IQ test forming an important component. Those who did well (about 20 percent) went on to grammar schools where they had the opportunity to continue a highly academic education up to the age of 18. At that point they would have the chance to enter university and subsequently the professions. Those who did not do so well in the examination were destined for a secondary modern school where practical skills were taught and students were expected to take undemanding jobs and home management. In essence the system produced an educated elite by blocking the majority of children from the advantages of a higher academic education.

This educational policy was developed though a series of committees, and one of the most influential figures in this respect was the psychologist, Cyril Burt. Burt was a pioneer in the development and refinement of IQ testing, and produced convincing evidence that IQ was largely genetic in nature. (He also believed intelligence to be fixed around the age of eleven—hence the eleven-plus examination.) In other words, schooling would play only a small factor in enhancing intelligence. Far better therefore to select children who had naturally inherited an above average intelligence and give them a first class academic education, than to waste time on children whose IQ could be improved by only a few points.

In particular, Burt believed that the sorts of work people did, and the social class they occupied, were largely related to their IQ and, in turn, would be passed on to their children. Of course such a philosophy was not uncongenial to the ruling sections of a highly class-ridden nation, for, as the Victorian hymn put it,

The rich man in his castle,
The poor man at his gate,
He made them, high or lowly,
And ordered their estate.[9]

Of particular importance were Burt's studies on twins who had been separated and brought up by different families, and in different environments (a study he commenced a year before the "eleven-plus" examination was adopted). If nurture and education played a significant role in the development of IQ, then differing results would be expected from twins raised in different environments. In fact Burt's statistics showed that the IQs were almost identical, which clearly demonstrated that genetic inheritance was the overall dominant factor in intelligence. If anyone had hitherto doubted Burt's claims on the genetic importance of intelligence these results put an end to the debate and, in 1946, Burt received a knighthood for his work.

In this way an entire educational policy was based on what appeared to be strict scientific research carried out by one of the world's leading experts. And so for several decades a highly educated minority, coming in the main from the middle classes, dominated the structure of British society. (Children from the upper classes would mainly have attended private fee-paying schools—the English "public school"—while the vast majority of children in grammar schools would be from the middle class). It could be argued that Burt's results were so readily accepted, and a particular school policy implemented, because it was exactly what many psychologists and educators wanted to believe. After all, it was adopted within the context of a country dominated by "the old school tie"; one in which a person's accent could be a barrier to the entry into certain professions or social circles.

It was only after Burt's death in 1971 that some scientists became suspicious that his results may not have been so clear-cut after all. The doubts began in the context of his work with twins and then extended to his earlier results on the importance played by genetics in IQ. How, for example, had Burt been able to discover so many twins who had been separated and brought up by different families? And what of his two collaborators, Margaret Howard and J. Conway? Did they actually exist, or were they a fabrication of Burt? After all, if they were genuine scientists why had they not continued to publish on their own? A careful reexamination of Burt's data indicated that the most convincing results on IQ and inheritance had been fabricated and by 1976 he was officially accused of fabricating data to prove that intelligence was inherited. At the same time, a number of surveys had already showed that the eleven-plus examination was an inefficient selection tool and was in fact sending a large proportion of children to the wrong types of school. Today most psychologists would agree that an adult's IQ is in part determined by nurture (education and environment) and in part by genetic inheritance.

As a footnote to the issue of IQ and the way statistical results can be misinterpreted, or even manipulated for personal or political ends, take the case of a survey that showed that babies brought up on breast milk were more intelligent than those raised on bottled milk. Ah ha! thought the researchers, maybe there is something in breast milk that aids in the development of IQ. But then the thought struck them, could it be that women who choose to breast-feed may, on average, be slightly more intelligent than those who bottle-feed? If so then the milk has nothing to do with the development of intelligence, it is simply a genetic effect showing up in the statistics.

I should add here that the whole notion of the significance of IQ and intelligence tests themselves have also come into question. For example, psychologists have long argued that the tests show a strong cultural and social bias. Others claim that IQ is only one factor in a person's ability to lead a successful, productive and rewarding life. The term "Emotional Intelligence" has been proposed by some as yet another measure, one of several that, taken together, would give a more rounded picture of a person's overall potential.

The example of the eleven-plus is yet another case in which a rather simplified solution is imposed on a complex issue involving such factors as nature versus nurture, the role of education, social barriers, the nature of work and so on. It particular, it shows how easy it is for people to accept a simple solution that accords with their own prejudices, or does not force them to confront a major change in attitude. It also demonstrates yet again that tendency to adopt a sweeping "solution", based on a rather simple but convenient argument, which can then be applied on a vast scale.

The example of Cyril Burt points to yet another assumption so many people operate under; that is, one of having trust in science, a topic that will be treated in more depth in chapter 6 of this book, on Trust.[10]

Getting healthy, getting sick

Before World War II most hospitals had a "septic ward", caring for victims of blood poisoning. Blood poisoning occurs when a combination of bacteria and toxins enter the body following an injury or infection. The result is fever and eventually septic shock with a death rate of around 50 percent. Today these wards do not exist. The reason? The development of penicillin and other antibiotics in the 1940s.

If the death rate due to blood poising fell dramatically during the 1940s we would expect to see dramatic changes associated with other medical breakthroughs. If we look at earlier centuries, for example, we note that in 1796 Edward Jenner discovered a vaccine against smallpox. In 1846 William Thomas Morton demonstrated anaesthetic at Massachusetts General Hospital. In the 1860s Joseph Lister pioneered antiseptic medicine and argued that surgical wounds should be kept sterile. In this same period, doctors in England, Ireland and France developed new approaches to diagnosis, as well as improved knowledge about a variety of diseases. It would therefore be natural to believe that these discoveries and innovations should be reflected in medical statistics. Indeed, death rates did decrease—but the reason turns out to be subtler than the result of any particular medical advance.

Thomas McKeown has made a famous study of the decline in 19th-century mortality rates in Britain.[11] His conclusion was that this decline had little to do with improvement in medicine or public heath, but was the result of changing living conditions, in particular improvements in nutrition. While specific details of "the McKeown thesis" have come under criticism, there is good reason to believe that while medical advances are welcome, sanitation, lifestyle and nutrition play a far more significant role in a nation's health. Yet again we find that systems are much more subtle than we anticipate and what appears to be an obvious outcome or explanation may not be as clear as we originally thought.

In the light of what appears to be our sophisticated advances in medicine it is necessary to add a footnote to the story of blood poisoning. Following surgery, septicemia is now on the rise in ever more virulent forms. The reason is that antibiotic-resistant bacteria are increasingly found in hospitals. According to *The Guardian* newspaper for December 21, 2005, each year 100,000 hospital patients in the United Kingdom are infected with MRSA, a from of staphylococcus that is resistant to a number of antibiotics. The Office of National Statistics reported that in 2006, the "superbugs" MRSA and *Clostridium difficile* contracted in hospitals were named as the main or contributory factors leading to death on 8132 death certificates.

Inevitably new drug-resistant strains of bacteria will evolve as a result of the over-use of antibiotics. But that is only part of the story; the other is the decline in the standards of hygiene in hospitals. In this respect

Britain's health service has come under serious criticism. At one time hospitals employed their own cleaning staff, nowadays hospital cleaning is contracted out to the lowest bidder, the number of cleaners have halved, proper sanitation procedures are not always carried out, and even when people know that surfaces must be bleached, doctors and nurses continue to use the alcohol wipes that are insufficient to kill off MRSA. As a result, hospitals have become dangerous places to inhabit. Again "the McKeown thesis" appears to be operating; medicine continues to show great advances but hygiene and common sense are more important.

Indeed poor hygiene extends beyond medical care and appears to be part of the general disintegration of hospital standards. *The Observer* for August 12, 2007 carried a report of a survey of 173 British hospitals. Forty-six percent had poor standards of cleanliness in the kitchens to the point of infestations by mice and cockroaches, staff not washing their hands, food being kept at the wrong temperatures and meal trays being used to transport contaminated materials from wards.

Effects of the McKeown thesis are also found in infant mortality rates. Britain has the worst statistics in Europe with 6.1 babies out of 1000 dying before their first year. (Figures for the USA are 7.8 per thousand.) Compare this with 3.9 in Finland or 4.8 in France. Social scientists at Sussex University note the strong correlation between poverty and infant mortality. UNICEF put Britain in 20th place, out of 23 countries for infant poverty—worse than Poland, Hungary or Turkey. And, as discussed above, infections are another cause of death in infants. Where hospitals in other European countries exercise preventive strategies there is no overall policy in Britain.[12]

Building a school

It would be difficult to disagree with the notion that the education of young people is of great importance. Some feel that there is a spiralling situation in many developing nations that could be broken with better education. With education, more opportunities are open and individuals are more motivated to make creative contributions to their society and participate in governance by even the simple process of voting. An educated population can engage in such things as technology, engineering, medicine and so on. The key to such advancement begins with a basic schooling at an early age.

This was the philosophy of a couple that decided to raise money to build a school for a community in Africa.[13] However, it was only when they were part way towards completing this project that they heard from the community itself that it didn't want a school but a well. The local people pointed out that no physical building was required, for the children could be taught in the shade of trees. What was necessary to the community was water, and for this the children had to walk for several hours each day to carry water back to the village. But with a well the children need not spend their time fetching water.

Again a tiny shift in perception is required. From our Western perception the equation is inevitable—children must be educated. Where do you get your education? Answer: in school. So if you wish to educate children you must first build a school. Not so, said an African community. Again the lesson is that systems must be understood from the inside out, not from the outside in!

No more help today, thank you

To amplify that story of Africa let us look at the whole issue of international aid and loans. In researching and thinking about this book my attention was brought to a particularly paradoxical element: the role of the West in supplying aid to the Third World. On the one hand I know a number of doctors and other volunteers who spend part of each year offering their services in Africa and know that as individuals they are providing very valuable assistance. In addition my son, Jason, worked for Médecins Sans Frontières in Afghanistan, Indonesia and a number of African countries and is now with the African Malaria project for the International Red Cross in Geneva. I know from speaking with him how effective this program is.

On the other hand, time and time again I have met with experts who tell me that the aid programs provided by the West are producing social and economic damage in Africa and in some cases encouraging dependency and corruption. Robert Calderisi provides a particularly strong indictment in his book, *The Trouble with Africa: Why foreign aid isn't working.*[14] Calderisi was the World Bank's international spokesperson on Africa and paints a serious picture of the many problems caused by aid and international loans.

There is enormous poverty in Africa. According to GIEWS (Global Information and Early Warning System on Food) and FEWS (Famine Early Warning System) as of the start of June 2005 at least 27 million people from 33 countries are at risk in a massive hunger crisis gripping the African continent.[15] According to a 2001 World Health Report almost two-thirds of deaths in Africa were from communicable diseases all of which, including HIV/Aids, are preventable and most of which could be eradicated with a modicum of effort.[16] Ninety percent of all deaths from malaria occur on the African continent.

In 2000 the United Nations Millennium Summit introduced eight goals for Africa including health, education and cutting poverty in half by 2015. Stephen Lewis has been Canadian ambassador to the United Nations as well as the Secretary-General's special envoy to Africa for HIV/ Aids. In his book *Race against Time*[17] he argues that the international community has fallen desperately short of these goals and that an appalling gap remains between vision and reality. In fact, over the last 30 years the continent has lost half of its export market.

Likewise, in the 2002 Monterrey Consensus the G8 countries agreed that if 0.7 percent of the GNP of rich countries could be sent to Africa then many of these problems would be solved.[18] Yet six years later things seem no better. Why should this be? I spoke to people who had worked in aid programs, or had been investigating their effectiveness, and discovered an overall picture which very much mirrors the arguments of this book—it's all a matter of outsiders, without any real understanding of local conditions, deciding what it best for people. In some cases policy makers define what they feel to be a major problem that is Asia- or Africa-wide and then set down what they believe to be the solution. The next step is to throw a massive budget at the project. The result is to create a large-scale program that may stretch across an entire continent but ends up being totally cumbersome and inflexible. Such an approach fails to take into account the importance of the different social, economic and environmental conditions in various regions and countries. In other words there is no room for adaptation to local conditions and contexts.

And so aid officers from the West move into an area and tell the local community what they have decided to do. It may be the case that a community does not really want that type of program, but they tend to agree to it because they feel that by accepting aid they may be able to leverage some other advantage at a later date. There may also be a variety of conditions attached to the aid, which a poor country badly in need of money may be induced to accept.

I was told of examples where aid workers enter an area only to discover that, for example, what the local people really need is a water supply, but water is not in the mandate of that particular aid organization. Their response is that "We can't do that but we'll go back and lobby for you." The hopes of the community are raised but in many cases nothing happens. There are yet other examples of projects that may be well meaning but where the country in question simply does not possess an infrastructure necessary to make an effective change.

Then there is the entire issue of accountability. Who determines if a program is effective and how? And what accountability is there going to be for the money poured into programs and of the competence of the officials involved? There are cases when an official initiates a program that turns out to be ineffective, but by then he or she has moved on to some other program and never experiences a career down-turn. What is more, the bureaucracy involved in accepting aid is staggering. Tanzania, for example, has to produce 2,400 reports each quarter and host 1,000 meetings with donors.

In an article in *Maclean's* magazine for January 2007 Larry Krotz points out that while the West is sending its experts to Africa, at the same time there is a substantial brain drain of educated Africans moving to the West. In fact, around 30 percent of Africa's university-trained professionals do not remain in the continent. That means between 50,000-70,000 African PhDs are now working in North America. Likewise if it were not for Zambians and Zimbabwean nurses (their training gives them more all-round skills than current Western programs) the British health service would collapse!

In the late 1970s the World Bank proposed a program of generous aid to Tanzania to enter into the world of light manufacturing. This included a plan to open a shoe factory with the crazy notion that it would be capable of underselling Italian shoemakers in their own market! After one year in operation the factory had exported nothing and was operating at only four percent capacity. What is more, the loan had to be repaid and this meant that the money would be coming out of the pockets of the country's farmers.

The overall result, according to some estimates, is that the cost of accepting foreign aid is probably about equal to its benefits, and in some cases worse. And what is more, countries can become dependent on aid, a state of affairs that robs them of their initiative. Generous donations of aid or loans to African countries can also foster corruption when funding finds its way into numbered Swiss bank accounts. In 2003, for example, the Nigerian authorities sued the British government in order to ensure their assistance in recovering the $5 billion stolen by a previous dictator, General Abacha. At present about 40 percent of African savings are located outside the country rather in African banks where they could help to stimulate the economy.

Calderisi suggests that lying behind many aid programs is a shared sense of guilt on the part of the West; guilt about a colonial past and guilt that people in the West have a high standard of living while those in other countries are malnourished and subject to terrible diseases. His conclusion is uncompromising: Africa does not need more direct aid but less. Most aid programs offer false hopes; they make countries dependent and discourage local initiatives. His suggestion is that aid should be cut to most African countries by 50 percent, but with the implication that leaner budgets would be more effectively managed. In addition, all ministers, senior officials and heads of state should open their bank accounts to public scrutiny. Countries that decline to do this, or refuse to hold internationally supervised elections, should not receive aid. In this way Africans themselves will be strongly motivated to push for internal reforms.

But while Calderisi proposes that the overall money spent on aid should be reduced, he nevertheless argues that more direct encouragement should be given to those countries that are truly serious about reducing poverty and improving their economies. The countries he identifies in his book, Uganda, Ghana, Mozambique, Tanzania and Mali, have developed their own self-directed programs. They do not need to be micromanaged by the West and in effect should be given blank cheques in order to continue with their own policies.

There is also the question of repayment of loans made to Africa by the West. Everyone from pop stars to the Pope are pleading that these loans should be forgiven. But what about other countries that had crippling problems and at the same time have found ways of paying back international loans. Indonesia found ways of restructuring in order to pay back its debts and so wonders why it was not "forgiven" when countries in Africa are. As we shall see later in this book, the system of microloans developed by Yunus and his Grameen bank clearly demonstrate that it is the poor who are the best at paying back their loans, while the rich find ways of diverting and leaking money away. Thus how much of a loan goes to buy food for the desperately poor and how much is diverted into other projects or the pockets of corrupt politicians?

Before we leave the question of aid let us look at just one example in greater detail and that is malaria. Malaria is spread by mosquitoes and causes an extensive number of deaths in many areas of the world. With the synthesis of the insecticide DDT in the early 1940s it became possible to eliminate mosquitoes and led to the Swiss chemist Paul Hermann Müller being awarded the 1948 Nobel Prize in medicine. The results of spraying with DDT were dramatic in reducing incidence of the disease. However during the late 1960s, and in particular following Rachel Carson's book *Silent Spring*, the tide began to turn against the use of DDT. It was argued that DDT resistant strains of mosquitoes had started to appear, and that the insecticide was spreading throughout the food chain resulting in such things as the thinning of bird eggshells and its appearance in human breast milk. In 1972 the United States banned the use of DDT and this ban then spread to other countries through the seventies and eighties— the UK finally banned DDT in 1984. As a consequence, the number of deaths caused by malaria began to rise and has become a very serious issue in Africa and other countries.[19]

Clearly the issue of malaria must be addressed and it is here that the West can offer assistance. The Canadian Red Cross has distributed millions of mosquito nets in Africa. These are impregnated with an insecticide that resists many washings. In the main this program has proved effective, if not 100 percent ideal, for in some cases the nets are used for fishing and in others cases people refuse to sleep under a net. Yet all in all this appears to be a case in which aid from the West is proving sensible and effective.

But let us look at the United States' $300 million malaria project for Africa. Calderisi points out that for every dollar spent on the program, one cent went to medicine, one cent to insecticides, six cents to mosquito nets and ninety-two cents to administration, training and research. Most of this last item found its way into the pockets of consultants from the West!

Now all this is not to say that money and programs are not required in areas of Africa and Asia. No, supplies, funds, expertise and services are badly needed but the key is to make these available when invited. We need to listen to what local people say, to learn about the cultures involved and to tailor aid programs in intelligent and creative ways that are appropriate to particular situations, individual needs and local customs and societies.

A report on the Voluntary Service Overseas' website,[20] posted on August 14, 2007 underlines this problem. Its director, Judith Brodie, cautioned young people that it may be more use for them to travel and see something of other communities in the world than to work abroad as volunteers. "We are increasingly concerned about the number of badly planned and supported schemes that are spurious," she wrote. Her warning was addressed in particular to "gappers", those who have graduated from college and would like to do some volunteer work in a "gap year" before enrolling at graduate school or settling down to steady employment. Last year VSO had warned that gappers risked becoming the new colonialists if attitudes to voluntary work in the developing world did not change. Indeed the gap year market was increasingly catering to the needs of volunteers, rather than the communities they claim to support.

But it is not just the West that is damaging Africa with aid and handouts. Now China has entered the picture with a pledge of $20 billion to finance trade and infrastructure in the continent. Zambia, for example, will receive $800 million over the next few years. But what are the spin-offs of this generous assistance? The town of Kabwe is the capital of the Zambian Central Province and the Mulungushi Textiles factory was the town's biggest employer. Opened over twenty years ago it turned out millions of yards of brightly colored cloth. Today the machines are silent as Chinese companies buy up the raw cotton for their own textile industry. As Wilfred Collins Wonani, who leads the Kabew Chamber of Commerce, says "We are back where we started. Sending raw materials out, bringing cheap manufactured goods in. This isn't progress. It is colonialism."

And while China's need for raw materials is certainly increasing revenues in Africa, they are also exporting huge volumes of manufactured goods to that continent. The effect is to compromise Africa's ability to improve its manufacturing capabilities and develop diverse economies. While Felix Mutati, Zambia's minister of finance, asks "Why should we have a bad attitude toward the Chinese when they are doing all the right things? They are bringing investment, world-class technology, jobs, value addition. What more can you ask for?" A member of the Zambian opposition, Michael Sata, puts it this way. "Their interest is exploiting us, just like everyone who came before. They have simply come to take the place of the West as the new colonizers of Africa."[21]

The whole story

Several of the examples within this book involve interventions and imposed solutions that have produced quite disastrous results. But having said this, the implication is that with the benefit of time we can look back to a situation, analyze it at leisure, and produce the true story of what occurred and what really should have been done. In fact this is another illusion we sometimes labour under—the assumption that we can always come up with an objective version of events in the past, and produce a neutral and comprehensive history of the facts in question. Unfortunately that is not always the case. It may be an old maxim that if we don't learn from history we are doomed to make the same mistakes, but it is often the case that history itself is incomplete.

The Japanese writer, Ryunosuke Akutagawa, produced a short story, "Rashomon"[22] in which a bandit rapes a woman and murders her husband, a Samurai warrior. The story is told, from the perspectives of several people: a woodcutter who found the body, a priest who saw the Samurai and woman before the event, the bandit who claims that the woman readily gave herself sexually to him and that the Samurai was killed in a duel, and from the perspective of the woman who claims she was raped. In addition, the Samurai gives his own version through a medium. Finally the woodcutter admits that he has lied and in fact witnessed the murder. But he is interrupted by a commoner who also claims to have witnessed the event. While "Rashomon" was published back in 1915, it very much expresses our postmodern attitude that there is no true objectivity to events and that each of us sees the world through our own particular filters.

In spite of this lack of objectivity claimed by Ryunosuke we continue to watch the news on television and read the newspapers, under the assumption that they will provide us with an objective account of events in the world. Some of us also read biographies believing they will provide us with an accurate account of a person's life and motivations. In this sense we all rely on the subject of chapter 6, trust. We place some level of trust in what newspapers, television news, history books and biographies tell us. But here it should be admitted that some people buy more than one newspaper to get a range of opinion, or acknowledge that the newspaper they are reading will generally display a particular political bias.

Let us turn to biography for a moment. Some years ago I wrote a biography of the American physicist, David Bohm.[23] In carrying out research for the book I interviewed his relatives, colleagues and friends, as well as reading letters and other documents. I was surprised at the different versions and anecdotes of events in his life and made it a rule that I would only include material that came from two independent sources, or from written documents. To take but one example; as a student Bohm had been very interested in the Russian social experiment with Marxism and for several months was a member of the Communist Party. Several people who had been Bohm's associates during that period, as well as a document Bohm had presented to the US authorities confirmed this, plus Bohm's own informally tape-recorded memoirs. However, while working on the book I received a letter from someone who had been one of Bohm's closest colleagues during that time. The letter emphatically denied that Bohm had ever had an association with Communism and asked me to bring this to the attention of the general public!

It is generally taken for granted that the police show great restraint in a potential confrontation to ensure that people are not injured. In particularly this should be true of the British police, who normally do not carry guns and have been known for their tact and even-handedness—the traditional bobby on the beat. Yet this does not appear to accord with the fact that, on July 22, 2005, plainclothes police officers rushed into the compartment of a London Underground train and shot a seated and totally innocent unarmed passenger, Jean Charles de Menezes, seven times in the head. Or that on June 2, 2006 they entered a house in Forest Gate, London and shot unarmed Abdul Kahar in the shoulder.

The background to these events involves terrorist attacks that had occurred in London, the assumption that de Menezes had been carrying a bomb, and that the house in Forest Gate contained a "chemical device". In researching this book I had intended to use these and other examples as cases in which the perception of complex situations was over simplified. However, the various newspaper and television accounts of both incidents were never that clear. In the de Menezes case some witnesses claimed that the man was running, that he jumped over a ticket barrier, and that he was carrying a bag that could have contained explosives. Others said that he was not carrying anything, that he had a normal travel pass, and even paused at the newspaper stand. Like Rashomon each witness saw a different series of events. Even Sir Ian Blair, the commissioner of the Metropolitan Police did not appear to know the story in any detail at the time. In a press conference held after the shooting Sir Ian told reporters that de Menezes' death was "directly linked" to anti-terrorist operations. It was only later that his officers informed him that de Menezes was a totally innocent member of the public who had been shot in error.

By 2008 the Metropolitan police were charged at the Old Bailey under Health and Safety Legislations. At the trial the prosecution alleged that a photograph produced by the police had been doctored. The judge, Mr Justice Henriques, told the jury: "A serious allegation has been made that a picture has been manipulated so as to mislead." The photograph involved was a composite showing de Menezes on the right and the terrorist Hussain Osman on the left. The two faces appeared very similar and could account for a case of mistaken identity. Clare Montgomery QC, for the prosecution said that it had been altered "by either stretching or resizing so the face ceases to have its correct proportions". The Metropolitan Police was fined £175,000 and ordered to pay £385,000 costs by trial judge Mr Justice Henriques.[24]

By November of the same year the Independent Police Complaints Commission (IPCC) inquiry had completed its hearings yet inconsistencies in "the whole story" still remained. For example, the eight police officers that entered the train all claimed to have shouted that they were "armed police" but none of the seventeen witnesses who were in the compartment recalled ever hearing such a warning. Only more than two years later did the IPCC publish its final report on the incident.[25]

I had also intended to give an account of the events at Waco, Texas in which the Bureau of Alcohol, Tobacco and Firearms raided the Branch Davidian compound in Texas on February 29, 1993, but again there appeared to be no definitive and objective report of what occurred. Who fired first—the Davidians, or the agents from the Bureau? The result was a siege that lasted for 51 days until, on April 19, tear gas was used and 80 Branch Davidians, including 22 children, died in a subsequent fire. But what caused the fire, and were the Davidians less able to escape because of the effects of tear gas? Accounts vary and the Internet is filled with any number of "true accounts" and conspiracy theories. A similar series of "accounts" can be found in the events leading up to the Jonestown mass suicides on November 18, 1978 in which over 900 people died, as well as the beating of Rodney King that led to the Los Angeles riots of 1992.

As a particular example of the difficulty in gathering a definitive account, take the beating of King by police officers that was videotaped by a bystander, George Holliday. This clearly shows the amount of violence used that resulted in eleven skull fractures, broken bones and teeth, kidney injuries, and permanent brain damage. However, what was not taped were the incidents that led up to the beating. Police alleged that King was extremely dangerous, probably on a drug such as Angel Dust, was not even subdued by a Taiser and lunged for one of the officer's weapons. However, there is no clear and independent evidence that this was the case.[26]

The examples above may be of extreme incidents, but it is clear that people's perception of events they have witnessed vary to the point where official accounts can be ambiguous. The conclusion is that hindsight may not always be an advantage. Situations are complex and our perceptions are deeply influenced by our backgrounds and the context in which we experience events. When we attempt to make interventions some of those interventions are helpful, some make a situation even worse. But even after the fact it may still not be that clear what really should have been done.

Reflections on Chapter 3

1. Make your own list of the "unexpected side effects" that you know of and begin to collect and reflect on examples of how an intervention in your community, business or social organization went wrong. What was

the reason? And given this knowledge how would you be able to design a more appropriate action?

2. Try to see the documentary *Darwin's Nightmare* about the Nile perch and reflect on the damage we may be doing right now to our planet.

3. Read Stewart Brand's book *The Clock of the Long Now* (London: Phoenix, 2000) in which he argues that decisions we are taking now will have repercussions not simply for decades but even for centuries and millennia. Take some time to reflect on what sorts of decisions and actions could have a long-term impact on our lives and the planet. Some may be easy to list, such as climate change and genetic engineering. Others may be subtler. If you had been around when the ARP net had been put into place could you have anticipated the enormous power the Internet would bring?

4. Saving money on hospital cleaning has resulted in the spread of deadly viruses. Try to find out how money is being spent in your community and city. Is it being spent wisely? If you think not, then it what ways could you, your friends, or the organizations to which you belong, make a change? Do you feel an individual can really make a difference to any situation or only when the time is right?

5. What are the issues about which you feel passionately—climate change, environmental pollution, poverty, famine, endangered species, homeless children, inner city violence, drug use, crime, etc? What can you do about this: Take some sort of action? Donate money? Join a group? Why not discuss how you feel about this with others.

6. And how much do you know about the complexities of those situations and how easy is it to find information? And what about those big news stories we read in the newspapers or see on television—how well are they reported? Do you feel you are getting the "whole story" or are the stories angled to fit a particular political agenda or to appeal to audience numbers? And think back to some of the "big stories" of the past couple of years—do you really know how they ended, how they were resolved, or did some other "big story" take over the news headlines? And what about the "small stories" of people and actions that make a difference, are they ever covered? If you have one share it with us. www.gentleaction.org.

Notes

1. The story of Thomas Midgley and his pioneering of Freon and leaded gas can be found in F. David Peat, *From Certainty to Uncertainty: The story of science and ideas in the twentieth century* (Washington, DC: Joseph Henry Press, 2002).

2. Much has been written about the Green Revolution and a great deal of information is available on the Internet, such as the website http://www.goodnewsindia.com and http://www.iisc.ernest.in/insa/ch21.pdf. In addition, for an overview of Indian agriculture see the report of the Indian Institute of Science at http://www.iisc.ernet.in/insa/ch21.pdf.

Of particular interest is Pat Roy Mooney, *Seeds of the Earth* (Ottawa: Inter Pares, 1980).

3. A.N. Wilson, *The Victorians* (London: Arrow Books, 2003).

4. Donated clothing. This story is discussed and debated on a number of websites related to aid in Africa. See for example http://ethanzuckerman.com/blog/2004/03/30/donated-clothing-as-an-economic-force/.

5. Tower blocks. See for example the Museum of London's website for www.museumoflondon.org.uk/English/EventsExhibitions/Past/Archive97-00/TowerBlocks.htm and other discussions on that website.

6. Discussion with Ernesto Sirolli.

7. Nile perch see, for example, "Lake Victoria: A sick giant" by Nancy Chege on http://cichlid-forum.com and the documentary film *Darwin's Nightmare* by Hubert Sauper.

8. From a series of discussions between Native American Elders and Western Scientist organized by Leroy Little Bear and F. David Peat.

9. "All Things Bright and Beautiful" text by Cecil Frances Alexander from *Hymns for Little Children*, 1848.

10. See for example, Sir Cyril Burt, "The Examination at Eleven-Plus", *British Journal of Educational Studies*, Vol. 7, No. 2 (May, 1959), pp. 99-117; Stephen Murdoch, *IQ: A Smart History of a Failed Idea* (Indianapolis: Wiley, 2007). A book that explores the evidence for and against Burt is N.J. Mackintosh, *Cyril Burt: Fraud or Framed* (Oxford: Oxford University Press, 1995).

11. "Reasons for the decline of mortality in England and Wales during the nineteenth century", *Population Studies* 16 (1962), 94-122. Further discussion of the McKeown thesis can be found in Simon Szreter, "The Importance of social intervention in Britain's mortality decline c.1850-1914: a re-interpretation of the role of public health", *The Society for the Social History of Medicine*, 1 (1): 1-38, 1988.

Trust in science and the founding of the Royal Society came from discussions with the historian of science, Michael Bresalier, who also pointed me to the Thomas McKeown thesis. This topic was also discussed during my period as a consultant for the Science Council of Canada.

An interesting exploration of the role of trust in science can be found in Steven Shapin, *A Social History of Truth: Civility and science in seventeenth-century England* (Chicago: Chicago University Press, 1994).

Information on MRSA comes from *The Guardian* newspaper for December 21, 2005.

12. For infant mortality statistics see, for example, http://www.cdc.gov/omhd/AMH/factsheets/infant.htm. See also papers posted on the University of Sussex website http://www.sussex.ac.uk/education and the UNICEF website www.unicef.org/media/media_pr_infantmortality.html.

13. This story was told to be by the couple involved.

14. Robert Calderisi, *The Trouble with Africa: Why foreign aid isn't working* (New York: Palgrave Macmillan, 2006).

15. http://medilinkz.org/healthtopics/nutrition/nutrition.asp, accessed March 4, 2008.

16. http://medilinkz.org/Features/Articles/dec2002/AfricaHealth2002.asp, accessed March 4, 2008.

17. Stephen Lewis, *Race Against Time* (Toronto: Anansi, 2005). Additional information on Africa comes from Dan Bortolotti, *Hope in Hell*, (Tichmond Hill, Ontario: Firefly Books, 2004).

18. 2002 Monterrey Consensus, http://www.l20.org/publications/12_L9_multilat_desai.pdf.

19. Wikipedia offers a popular account of the history of DDT, active debate continues and many references can be found on the Internet. http://en.wikipedia.org/wiki/DDT.

20. See VSO's website http://www.vso.org.uk.

21. Reported by Lydia Polgreen, and Howard W. French from Addis Ababa, *New York Times*, August 21, 2007.

22. Ryunosuke Akutagawa, *Rashomon and Other Stories* (North Clarendon, VT: Tuttle, 2007).

23. F. David Peat, *Infinite Potential: The life and times of David Bohm* (Reading, MA: Addison-Wesley, 1997).

24. Sky News website, www.sky.com/news, for October 17 and November 1, 2008.

25. Sky News website, www.sky.com/news, for November 8, 2008.

26. Robert Gooding-Williams, (ed.), *Reading Rodney King/Reading Urban Uprising* (London: Routledge, 1993).

Chapter 4.
Rigidity

At 2.30 a.m. on the morning of September 26, 1997, an earthquake hit close to the town of Assisi in Italy. Six hours later, as clergy and art experts were inspecting damage to the frescoes in the Basilica of St Francis, a second quake occurred bringing down part of the ceiling, killing four people and further damaging the frescoes. The building had stood for eight hundred years and had been subject to more than one earthquake. Why now had the ceiling fallen? The reason was not difficult to discover. The original ceiling consisted of plaster applied to wooden laths. It had been the type of structure sufficiently flexible to "give" and could therefore withstand earth tremors. More recently, however, engineers had decided to reinforce the ceiling with concrete. The result was that, when subjected to an earthquake, the concrete cracked and lost its integrity, collapsing with the second quake.

The issue was not that of strength but of rigidity. A rigid system may have strength and resistance, but is unable to give and yield. While it can easily withstand a weak stress, push it a little harder and it will suddenly give way. On the other hand, a flexible system is able to give and "go with the flow". After all, the Empire State Building actually sways in a high wind, and look at the way the wings flex on a jumbo jet. The Basilica has since been repaired using special flexible steel wires which will stretch and then return to their original positions in the event of any future earthquake.[1]

Something very similar occurs with organizations. A healthy organization is able to adjust to sudden changes, market stresses and so on, making a series of internal adjustments to meet a new environment and then returning to its original efficient state when the change has passed.

Rigid organizations, however, continue to function as before until they meet change in inappropriate ways. There are so many ways in which this rigidity is reinforced—a series of policies and mission statements that officials stick to in blind ways, a hierarchical organizational structure in which those below have been conditioned not to question orders from above, an organization in which there are no healthy feedback loops whereby information about the organization's behavior can flow both vertically and horizontally. Or one in which there are subdepartments and branches that don't effectively communicate with each other.

In fact organizations, businesses and politicians can exhibit many of the symptoms of mental illness. An organization can become autistic to the point where it is no longer capable of "reading" the messages that are being sent by the public or society at large. It can become schizophrenic when its internal representation of, for example, the marketplace does not match the reality outside—in other words, it has delusions and hallucinations about the way a market or an economy is working. Its reactions to change become entirely inappropriate, its thinking becomes blunted and inflexible.

In considering rigidity we must remember that an organization has both a formal and an informal structure. Its formal structure will involve its CEO, board, managers, team leaders and so on, with instructions flowing downwards from the board, and additional information flowing back upwards. There may also be horizontal and diagonal flows of information and instructions. This structure may even be reflected in the physical organization of the actual building or office, with CEO and senior managers located at the top of the building and general office workers at the bottom.

But an organization also has an informal structure in which valuable exchanges are made at the water cooler or photocopier, over coffee breaks, during lunch and on the golf course. An organization remains flexible and creative to the extent to which these exchanges take place, and the extent to which senior management is part of this process.

I know of a research institute in Canada in which the president used to occupy the same building as his research teams. Each day he would drop in on one of these teams during their coffee break and chat with them. He would find out, on the floor, the general mood of the group, how their research was progressing, what difficulties they were encountering and if they needed any assistance. The atmosphere at that time was highly creative, executive decisions could be made rapidly and individuals felt they were part of a highly motivated team.

But then changes were made and a separate administrative building opened, with the president and vice-presidents on the top floors and various administrators, secretaries and accountants below. No longer did the president drop in during coffee breaks, no longer did he have an intimate and immediate contact with his research teams. Indeed, it became increasingly difficult to speak to the president, for researchers were being filtered through his assistants and vice presidents. While the formal structure of the organization remained the same—the chain of command had not changed—the informal structure of flexible exchange had been compromised. As a result, people began to feel increasingly disconnected from the organization and some of the most talented scientists found jobs elsewhere. A visitor during that period remarked, "Do you know the difference between this place and the Bell Labs? Here you don't see any lights on in the labs after six in the evening. In the Bell Labs people are still working after ten at night!"*

Contrast this with Canada's Department of External Affairs under its Secretary of State, Mitchell Sharp. While its building on Sussex Drive in Ottawa had an executive dining room, Sharp used to line up in the ground floor cafeteria with maintenance workers, secretaries and other staff. It was a truly democratic gesture which brought him in close contact with every level of his department.

Heroes and clowns

The rigid response is also embodied in the notion of the so-called "robust encounter"— another way of saying you are trying to make your point in the most forceful way possible. In his book, *The Comedy of Survival*,[2] Joseph Meeker argues that our conventional Western approach to situations is to take the heroic route. The hero uses force and does battle. He is the lone individual who must combat superior odds. Greek theatre is full of heroes, and today many films are about heroes who say in aggressive tones such things as "Go ahead, make my day". It is this same "heroic" approach that I see operating in our modern world as politicians and organizations *battle* against what they see as the problems that constantly face them. It is also present in the many metaphors we employ: "war on want", "war on drugs", "war on crime", "war on terrorism", while doctors take "aggressive measures" against disease and employ the "magic bullets" of drugs, with patients either "winning the battle" or "losing the fight" against disease.

But, as Meeker points out, other cultures do not necessarily give so much honour to the hero. Some favour the path of comedy. Comedy is associated with characters who break the rules and cross boundaries. Comedy is about changes in identity, tricksters, ambiguity and the transformation of roles. While tragedy inevitably ends in death, comedy ends in marriage, the continuity of society, and fertility. Clearly more

---

* The Bell Labs are located in Murray Hill, New Jersey and its researchers have earned six Nobel prizes.

comedy is needed in our world, so maybe Tina Turner was right when she sang "We don't need another hero."

Universities

A few years ago we organized a conference here in Pari on the future of universities. Participants came from North America, several European countries and Australia, so it is fair to say that we had a good representation of a variety of educational systems. However, the overall picture painted was fairly uniform. People were not happy in their universities. They felt that, as organizations, they had become overly rigid. They seemed to be run by administrators and accountants, rather than researchers and educators. Students were not viewed as young minds to be opened to new ideas, taught to think critically, and to engage fruitfully in the search for knowledge. No, they were clients that needed to be satisfied, and professors were therefore to be judged on how much satisfaction they gave to these clients. Even academic topics were chosen, not so much for the valuable knowledge they contained, but for the potential job skills they conveyed. Those topics that did not provide an easy vehicle towards employment were dismissed from the syllabus as "orchid disciplines".[3]

Universities were once supposed to be the repositories of knowledge for society, a place in which new ideas were generated that could be passed on to future generations. Now they had become degree factories through which a person passed on their way to, hopefully, a lifetime of employment. How ironic therefore that, David Schrum, a student of mine should receive his PhD diploma in an envelope with a customs declaration marked "Degree Certificate. No commercial value".

Global warming and Chernobyl

Global warming is generally acknowledged to be a serious threat to our planet. We know that if it is not checked, melting ice caps will cause a rise in sea levels that would result in the flooding of major seaboard cities. Other threats include a possible change in the great conveyor belt of the Gulf Stream which would, paradoxically, plunge Northern Europe into an Ice Age—after all England is at the same latitude as Hudson Bay and Norway and Sweden as that of Greenland!! Another phenomenon, global dimming (tiny emission particles in the upper atmosphere that act as nuclei around which water can condense), holds the danger that the monsoons that irrigate the Indian subcontinent could fail and produce widespread famine.

There has been much talk about abandoning fossil fuels for heating, using hydrogen for cars, and turning to wind, solar and tidal power. But many experts feel that this conversion will be too slow and in the short term we must rely upon nuclear power as a stopgap measure. Indeed the energy policy adopted by the British government in 2006 involved a program of building new nuclear power stations. The case for nuclear power has also been strongly argued by James Lovelock in his book *The Revenge of Gaia*.[4] Of course the general public are wary of nuclear power, so Lovelock points to its long safety record in the USA and UK. But here I feel he is being a little disingenuous, for it is not so much that nuclear power is inherently safe, because reactors are well designed and protected by all sorts of safety measures, but that the main countries using nuclear power, such as Canada, the USA, Britain and France have a strong cultural history of concern with safety and an impressive technological background. Running a nuclear power station is in some ways no different from running a railway, a fleet of aircraft or a hospital. It demands highly trained and responsible individuals, who work within a system that is both robust and flexible, and who live in a culture that is not associated with widespread corruption and bribery. Yes, the CANDU reactor used in Canada may be a safe design, but put the same reactor in a country rife with corruption and willing to cut corners and it could be a recipe for disaster.

With that in mind let us look at what happened at Chernobyl on April 26, 1986. There have been a number of analyses of the Chernobyl nuclear disaster. (And here keep in mind my earlier caution that we may never know "the whole story".) In part it arose out of what has since been called a design fault in the RBMK type of reactor used, one in which instabilities can cause a rapid power increase. Where other reactors had inbuilt safeguards, these were absent from the Chernobyl reactor. But a far more interesting cause, from the perspective of this present book, is the absence of a "safety culture"; one which would allow the reactor to operate in a safe way. There is evidence that the reactor manufacturer did not inform the plant operators that the system could become unstable at low power. Moreover, the director of the plant had previously managed a coal-fired plant, his chief engineer also came from a conventional power plant, and the other plant operators had little or no experience of nuclear reactions. In short, this created an atmosphere in which, during a test of the reactor, a number of mistakes were made. Safety procedures were ignored and there was a breakdown in communication between those responsible for running the reactor and those conducting the test.

As we have seen the safe running of aircraft, trains, hospitals and nuclear reactors depends not only on a variety of inbuilt electronic and mechanical safeguards but on the integrity of an underlying organizational structure, one in which there is good communication and everyone is aware of his or her responsibilities. When this is missing even the best safety features and back-up procedures are at some point going to fail. In Chernobyl a series of mistakes led to a sudden power surge 100 times above normal. The corresponding jump in temperature caused the fuel rods to rupture, and when the hot fuel hit the cooling water it caused an explosion that destroyed the reactor core. As a result over 300,000 people had to be evacuated and large areas were badly contaminated.[5]

I would certainly accept Lovelock's argument that nuclear power in inherently safe—but that safety very much depends on it being embedded in a technologically sophisticated culture that is never willing to cut corners.

An interesting example of the way the integrity of a human-designed system ultimately dependent on the effectiveness of the human infrastructure that surrounds it surfaced in a series of television news reports (BBC news and SKY news) starting in November 2007 just as I was putting the finishing touches to this chapter. It revolved around the loss of a CD-ROM containing the personal data of millions of British people and created a scandal that caused uproar in the House of Commons.

The origin of this case lay several years ago when it was decided to create a central database that would contain medical and social records for every British citizen, in addition to such things as police and court records. Eventually this system was to extend right across Europe. The justification was that of speed and efficiency. Take, for example, the hypothetical case of a Londoner who becomes involved in a serious traffic accident in Madrid. Using this system doctors in the Emergency Room can rapidly obtain medical data on their patient including possible drug allergies, blood type and outstanding medical conditions that may be relevant to the case.

I remember talking to one of the people who was setting up this system and he assured me that it was totally secure. The computer system was designed in such a way that the public had no need to worry about data theft or hackers. However, while the overall design and safeguards of the computer system may be excellent, computers themselves are operated by human beings who may be far more casual in their approaches.

The particular incident that burst into public notice involved an employee who had made two CDs containing copies of personal data including the names, bank and National Insurance Numbers of 25 million Britons. The discs were sent by courier and did not arrive at their destination. This followed on from an earlier report of a laptop being stolen which contained data on individuals from the British Inland Revenue department. By November 21 the Chancellor of the Exchequer was apologizing to an angry opposition and the chairman of HM Revenue and Customs Paul Gray announced his resignation. In the days that followed additional reports began to leak out that indicated employers were walking around with data copied onto their memory sticks, and putting data discs in the trunks of their cars when they drove to meetings or other buildings and on November 24 it was admitted that an additional six CDs containing data had gone missing. The highly expensive computer system itself was secure but the infrastructure around it was totally leaky.

A similar problem occurred in the United States as an article in the *Washington Post* for March 24, 2008 explains. In February of that year a laptop containing sensitive medical information on 2,500 patients was stolen. In this particular case the data was not even encrypted, in violation of federal data-security policy. To make matters worse it was almost a month before patients were informed that their medical records had been compromised—the reason given was that the agency did not wish to cause panic. Indeed as with the UK this is by no means an isolated case since the US Government Accountability Office found that 19 out of 24 agencies that had been reviewed had experienced breaches in which personal information became at risk for identity theft.

The individual

The spectrum from rigidity to flexibility not only operates within an organization but at the level of the individual. It can, for example, spell the difference between a good speaker and a boring one. How many times have I been to a conference where speakers read from their papers? The voice is monotonous and I would much rather have been given the lecture to read over coffee than be forced to sit in the hall and listen. The problem is that the talk was written days or weeks ago. The speaker is in no way responding to the context of the conference, to the mood and level of the audience, and to what has been said by previous speakers. A good teacher, or speaker, will have jotted down a series of headings. They will get a "feel" for the audience, and for its particular level of interest.

They will be willing to change direction, respond to a mood, insert a little humour, even respond to a question while in midstream. They know that the best they can do is have their audience take a few points away with them once the conference has ended, and the way to do that is to engage the audience, bring them in, respond in a human way with warmth and enthusiasm.

Flexibility is also the mark of a good performer, be it an actor, singer or pianist. A person may have been acting Hamlet for several weeks, or performing a Beethoven piano concerto for the umpteenth time but that night, as every night, they have to bring something new to the performance. They must have the audience breathing with them, they have to listen and respond to the other actors and performers around them. They have to deliver "To be or not to be" as if people were hearing it for the very first time, and as if those thoughts were appearing freshly minted in Hamlet's mind. Simply repeating a formula will not do, there must be internal flexibility and engagement.

But this is also demanded of the viewer, listener or reader. When we engage a work we must also take the responsibility of bringing it alive, of making it new. Round Christmas time I sometimes take Charles Dickens' *Pickwick Papers* from the shelf. It is a book I have read many times but with each reading it is I who help to bring alive Mr Pickwick skating on the pond, Christmas dinner with the Wardles, the Fat Boy nodding off to sleep and Sam Weller's cockney humour. Again it is the creative encounter, the ongoing engagement that brings the world alive for us.

Fragmentation

Rigidity is also related to fragmentation, for when different parts of a system do not communicate well with each other they begin to break away from the whole and act independently, without taking into account the wider environment in which they operate. The result can be behavior that appears irrational when viewed in a more complete context.

Take for example an issue we have already touched on, global warming, which calls on us to reduce our use of fossil fuels. One way we can do this is to develop more rational transport systems in which we don't have the situation of a large number of individuals each one driving their own car or making a large number of short haul flights. Let me take a particular case. Recently I attended a conference in England that dealt, in part, with the environment. To my surprise some of the participants had arrived by air. And by this I don't mean that they had flown the Atlantic to attend, but had made short trips of 200 or 250 miles within the United Kingdom. Now it certainly was not a matter of saving time, for Britain has a high speed train system, most cities have a centrally located station and one can turn up a few minutes before the train leaves and have no need to wait at a baggage carousel at the other end. So why fly? The simple reason is that in so many cases it is much cheaper to fly than to take the train, since trains in Britain are the most expensive in Europe. In England I can make a train journey of only 28 miles for 19 euros, but for the same fare I can travel 411 miles in France and 680 miles in Italy! [6]

But this is a totally crazy position. The British Government is keen to reduce its carbon emissions and at the same time allows for a transport system in which it is cheaper to drive your car or take short haul flights than it is to take the train! Environmentalists know about the perils of global warming, and that much larger carbon emissions per person and per mile are caused by flying than by taking the train. So why does a country allow this state of affairs to persist? Why not estimate the true cost of flights in terms of the potential for flooding and other aspects of climate change? (Europe's largest wind farm will be located in England's Lake District and used to produce electricity without making carbon emissions, but according to the environmentalist, George Monbiot, the amount of carbon saved in one day is offset by just three jumbo jets flying the Atlantic.) Clearly the whole issue of transportation in the United Kingdom has become fragmented.

Let me give another example, this time taken from Monbiot's book *Captive State: The corporate takeover of Britain*.[7] One of the arguments often used in suggesting how ordinary people can help reduce carbon emissions is to "eat locally". That means, not purchasing food that has been flown halfway across the world. But is it really that easy? Monbiot discovered that, sure enough, vegetables sold at two supermarkets in Worcestershire were grown just 2 km from the town. However they were first trucked 70 km to Herefordshire, and then an additional 130 km to a packing place in Wales. Finally they were driven to a distribution depot some 290 km away, and then a further 180 km to the supermarkets. Local vegetables grown 2 km away had travelled a total of 670 km from farmer to customer!

Our daily lives are so often filled with minor frustrations simply because a fragmented society does not behave in intelligent ways. What is more, only a very minor adjustment, and at very little cost, could change things in a positive way. Take the integration of transport, for example. I have praised Italy for its low cost of train travel. On the other hand I can take a forty minute bus ride from my village of Pari to the main railway station at Grosseto where I can then take the train to Rome. The morning train, however, leaves at 9.30 am, yet the bus arrives at the station at 9.32! How simple it would be to adjust the bus timetable to coordinate with the train, as is the case in some cities of North America.

In fact an integrated transport system already existed in the first half of the nineteenth century. Isambard Kingdom Brunel's visionary achievement began in London where passengers could drive by carriage right up to the Great Western Railway train in a covered area and have their cabin trunks placed in the guard's van while they entered their compartment. The train took them across Western England, along the railway Brunel had constructed, to the Bristol dockyards where they could then enter Brunel's Great Western steamship and sail to New York. In so many ways things seem to have gone backwards since then!

Perception

The way we view a system, a situation, a social group or an environmental issue is very much determined by our own personal history and the context in which our perception operates. Experiments have been done in which subjects are asked to look at a series of photographs while their eye movements are being scanned. After reading a piece of text—one that presents a particular context in which an image is about to be seen—the pattern of eye movements change. Depending on the nature of the text the subject will be searching for different sorts of information in the picture—in fact, they are essentially "seeing" a different scene. In yet another example, a series of faces are displayed and the subject is asked to select someone as a potential jury member, or identify who may have committed a crime. Subtle clues in the piece of text can easily direct a subject to pick out a certain face as being either suspicious or trustworthy.

So our ability to judge a situation, or make an intervention, is going to depend on the way we "see" that situation. The more we are aware of our prejudices, the more we can give attention to the context in which we are doing that seeing, the more unbiased the information we will be able to take in. This is of particular importance if we are required to make a rapid decision.

In his book *Blink: The power of thinking without thinking*,[8] Malcolm Gladwell gives examples of what he terms our innate power to "thin slice". In other words, to make rapid and accurate judgments using only small amounts of information. Readers of his book will probably remember his example of a supposed *kouros*, a statue of a young man, that was authenticated over a fourteen-month period by consultants to the Getty museum as being from ancient Greece. However when Evelyn Harrison, an expert on Greek sculpture, simply glanced at the sculpture she instinctively knew there was something wrong—it could not be authentic. She did not require months of study, or a laboratory analysis of the stone. She simply "knew" that something about it was wrong.

Gladwell also warns that while we can operate well on thin slices of information, there is always the danger that prejudice can distort the validity of our first impressions. In fact it was this insight that gave Gladwell the idea for the book itself. In an interview for the *Independent on Sunday* (March 19, 2006) he related what happened after he had allowed his hair to grow into an afro. He was walking down 14th Street in New York when he was jumped by three policemen and interrogated for twenty minutes. The police were looking for a rapist who in fact did not resemble Gladwell at all. However, the appearance of his hair simply blinded the police to the fact that his build, height and age were quite different. They were used to a particular context involving people with afros in New York and within that context they had ignored the other factors of Gladwell's appearance.

Let us return to the two incidents I referred to in the previous chapter in which the British police appeared to act out of character—the shooting of de Menezes on the London Underground, and the raid on a house in Forest Hill. Both incidents took place within a context that limited the police force's ability to perceive the important details of a situation and so ended up with a profoundly distorted picture of events. The reason was that only a few weeks earlier terrorist suicide bombings on the London Underground had left 52 people dead and more than 700 injured. Two weeks later there were more attempts which this time failed and the police believed that a number of suspects were still at large.

According to police intelligence, one of these suspects lived in a block of flats in Tulse Hill, London. A surveillance procedure was mounted, but at the moment the innocent de Menezes left the flats to go to work, the office involved had turned away to urinate. When de Menezes was seen walking along the road it was simply assumed that he was the subject involved. As he entered the Stockwell tube station perceptions became quite wild and eye witness accounts simply did not agree. What is more the armed officers who followed him into the station did not have cell phones that worked underground, and therefore could not contact a senior officer to indicate that the suspect was not wearing anything that would conceal a bomb and to confirm that they were still required to shoot him. As a result they entered the compartment where de Menezes was sitting quietly and shot him seven times in the head using hollow point (dum-dum) bullets.

What is true about an individual's perception, or that of a group of policemen, is even more the case when it comes to an organization which is assessing a situation that it sees as "a problem". If the organization is overly rigid then its perceptions are going to be similarly limited. Maybe it only "sees" the details, for example, and misses out on the larger picture. Or sees a wider context but misses some important detail. Here we can call on the example of human vision. The eye has an extremely sensitive area called the "yellow spot" that is capable of great discrimination. We may glance at a scene, scanning it with rapid eye movements and pick out a region of interest. The muscles surrounding the eye then direct it to bring that region over the yellow spot, a situation in which the object can be seen in much greater detail.

But there is one drawback to the yellow spot. While it provides great discrimination it is not so good at picking up movement. So while we are focussing on something in detail, we may miss the signals of an approaching predator. This movement is detected "out of the corner of the eye" and the brain immediately moves the eye to bring the suspected predator in focus over the yellow spot. So human vision needs two abilities—one which enables us to make a detailed examination of a portion of a scene, and the other that is able to set that particular portion within a wider context.

The philosopher A. N. Whitehead argued that the human mind works in a similar way. He spoke of *prehension*, as if the mind reaches out like a hand to touch, or even grab at, the world. Part of this function is the ability to make a detailed analysis of an idea or situation. But there is another function of the mind, one which seeks meaning and places the details of a situation within their wider context. Again both forms of mental perception are needed.

Likewise Carl Jung wrote of what he called our "rational functions". These are "thinking" and "feeling". The thinking function allows us to analyze and add up the pros and cons of taking a certain decision, while the feeling function tells us how we really feel about taking one or the other decision; what it means to us, and what value it has. Someone whose personality is dominated by the thinking function may reason that it makes sense to move and take a new job in a different city. The list they make of pros and cons is quite convincing, but a year later they may be quite unhappy without close friends and in a city they don't particularly like. On the other hand someone guided by the feeling function may impulsively move to a new job because they just know it is "tailor-made" for them. The job will be wonderfully satisfying at first, until they realize they have never taken into account that it means a two-hour drive in heavy traffic each morning, that they are not fully qualified to use the particular computer system involved, and financially they are now worse off than before. Again a balanced person must rely on using both functions together. They must weigh up advantages and disadvantages but also take into account the value and meaning of what they are doing in their lives—what sort of relationship they are starting or what sort of work they are taking on.

Human vision, Whitehead's prehension, and Jung's rational functions are just metaphors but they do indicate the importance of a balanced viewpoint if an individual or organization is going to have an accurate perception of situations around them, both in its important detail and within the wider context of society, the environment or the economy. And so the message of this chapter has been that organizations must be flexible and creative. They must respond to the world around them, but to do so in appropriate ways implies that their perceptions of the world are not distorted or fragmented. They must have an overall feel for the context in which they are operating, while at the same time give proper attention to daily details. For this to operate an organization must be creative and flexible drawing not only on the explicit skills of its managers and employees but also on their valuable tacit knowledge.

We have also seen in the specific example of nuclear safety that safeguards and good design are not by themselves sufficient, but that an infrastructure based on the free exchange of information and freedom from corruption and corner-cutting is essential. We could go even further than this and argue that one of the most important elements in any organization is that of trust and ethics. But since the whole issue of trust and ethics is such a wide-reaching topic it will be the subject of another chapter.

❧ Reflections on Chapter 4

1. As a member of an organization, or in your workplace, how easy is it to have your suggestions and proposals received? How does information flow? Is it bottom-up, top-down, horizontal or via a multiplicity of interconnected feedback loops? Are you happy working there and do you feel your presence makes a difference? How would you rate its flexibility or rigidity? If you are unhappy with the way it operates can you think of ways in which it would be restructured, and if this happened what would be the outcomes within the company or organization, and how would

it affect the other organizations with which it links? Make a flow chart diagram of information flows and discover where new ideas are being generated and how decisions are made.

2. What about your local community? Who actually runs things? How easy is it to make yourself heard? How easy would it be for your community to move in a new direction?

3. When you, your organization or your business, faces complex issues in the world at large—economic, social, political, etc—how easy it is for you to gather information? Do you have a clear perception of what is going on or are there are a number of biases that cause you or your organization to look only in a particular direction? How easy would it be for you to draw a flow chart of all the dynamics of a system you are dealing with? And how would that be mirrored within a flow chart of your own organization. Do they complement each other or are there areas of fracture where things are mismatched?

Remember to post your observations, experiences and questions on www.gentleaction.org.

Notes

1. See, for example, "When a Quake Strengthens a Basilica", *New York Times*, November 27, 1999.

2. Joseph W. Meeker, *The Comedy of Survival: Literary ecology and a play ethic* (Arizona: University of Arizona Press, 1997).

3. The state of universities can be found in our conference report at www.paricenter.com/conferences/academy/academy.php.

4. James Lovelock, *The Revenge of Gaia* (Cambridge, MA: Perseus, 2007).

5. See, for example, http://world-nuclear.org/info/chernobyl/inf07.htm. And for the environmental and human impacts, http://environmentalchemistry.com/yogi/hazmat/articles/chernobyl1.html.

6. Article on rail prices from *The Times*, November 19, 2004.

7. George Monbiot, *Captive State: The corporate takeover of Britain* (London: Macmillan, 2000).

8. Malcolm Gladwell, *Blink: The power of thinking without thinking* (London: Penguin, 2006).

Chapter 5.
Creative suspension

"There is a lot of fear in the markets. When there is fear, people have a tendency to overreact."

Bob Moulton, mortgage broker. *New York Times* "Quote of the Day", August 12, 2007.

Most people feel it incumbent upon themselves to take some form of action when things around are going badly wrong. If a child falls off a bicycle, a parent will cuddle and try to comfort the child. If someone drops their groceries we help to pick them up. These are simple acts of human generosity and kindness. On the other hand, these are all relatively simple situations with obvious solutions. But other cases can be more complex, to the point where even the most intelligent and intuitive person realizes that while something needs to be done, they are not at all clear as to what is the best and most appropriate form of action to take.

Under such circumstances individuals can be flexible and attempt to "feel out" the situation without necessarily imposing a solution or forcing some sort of action. But what of organizations, government and policies? They may be mandated to take action and therefore forced to move ahead without being fully aware of the consequences. And so in this chapter I am going to suggest something quite radical that I am calling "Creative Suspension"[1]. It is the voluntary act, on the part of an individual or organization, to suspend, if only for a moment, their normal "knee-jerk" reaction to rush in and "help" or "put things right".

Take as an example, a traffic accident. A layperson who is present may, on impulse, drag a victim from a car, cradle someone's head, pull a piece of metal out of a person's chest, or tie a tourniquet around a bleeding leg, and then rush off and leave the victim in order to attend to someone else. In each case their good intention may make an injury even worse: that tourniquet may be left on too long, dragging a person out of the car may increase internal bleeding, pulling out that piece of metal may cause a hemorrhage, and lifting the head of someone with a spinal injury could be disastrous. By contrast, ambulance personnel are trained exactly in how to approach the scene of an accident. The first step is to perform a triage and assess the relative seriousness of each victim's injuries. In other words, to suspend direct action until they have a clear idea of what has happened at the accident site. A person with blood all over his or her face may turn out to have only superficial cuts, someone sitting at the steering wheel with a dazed expression may be in shock or have a potentially serious head injury.

The very first step, as any doctor knows, it to use the eyes and observe the condition of a victim. Only when this is done will the medical personnel use touch. Finally, when a full assessment has been made, they will begin their interventions. This act of suspension may only take a few moments, but it is necessary to understand the situation in order to have a complete picture of each potential injury before determining who needs to be treated first, who can be moved, who can be left until later, and who must be rushed to the emergency room of the hospital.

Likewise, when emergency workers arrive at the scene of a fire or explosion they must first assess the structural integrity of the building before moving masonry and assisting victims—otherwise parts of the building could collapse and endanger the lives of both the injured inside and the emergency workers who are trying to help them.

Police officers who arrive at the scene of a hostage-taking or standoff remain calm and do not act in haste. The objective is to negotiate, to find a way out and ensure that the hostage is not killed.

This is what I am calling "creative suspension" and it is related to other approaches and techniques whereby unexamined assumptions and rigidities are brought into conscious awareness. For example, Sigmund Freud's notion of "non-judgemental listening" is common not only to psychoanalysis but also to various meditative practices. Artists, composers, scientists and other creative people often describe how their work unfolds from a form of creative "listening". These acts of listening and watchfulness have the effect of dissolving rigidities and rendering a system more flexible.

In the case of an ambulance crew or firefighters they are specifically trained to assess a situation before taking action. And again I want to stress that creative suspension is very different from "doing nothing". It is an active form of watchfulness and assessment in order to take the most effective action as quickly as possible. But what about a business, an aid organization or a social group that is faced with a crisis? Could they exercise a creative form of suspension when all their organizational instincts are to act, act, act? If they were simply to suspend this conditioned reflex then probably lights would begin to flash and alarm bells ring. There would be a sense of panic and chaos with a complex flow of commands and information. All of this would be not generated by any external threat but through the internal structure of the organization itself. But suppose an organization were to exercise a very sensitive and active form of suspension, while remaining sensitive to what is going on within. It this way it may be possible to become aware of the whole nature of the organization, of its values, the way its information flows, its internal relationships, dynamics and, in particular, where its fixed and inflexible responses lie—its organizational neuroses and psychoses if you like.

Something new and more flexible could be reborn out of the breakdown of fixed patterns in an organization, policy group, or individual. By means of a very active watchfulness it may be possible to detect unexamined presuppositions, fixed values and conditioned responses, and in this way allow them to dissolve by no longer giving energy to support them. The idea would be to permit the full human potential for creativity to flower within each individual in an organization. It would enable people to relate together in a more harmonious way and human needs and values to be acknowledged.

Self-Organized Creativity

Maybe this will become clearer if we return to the notion of self-organization. A traditional organization may be quite rigid and patterned in its operations. Its mission statement would have been written many years ago but even if times have changed this statement must still be adhered to. It has its hierarchy of control and well-established rules of procedure, which may have been set in place by a head office in some distant location. And so the organization's behavior remains the same year after year, even if the external context in which it operates may have changed. In this way the organization continues to persist—or becomes extinct.

By contrast a self-organized operation did not begin with a pre-established set of rules but emerged in a creative way out of the growth of feedback loops and flow-through of information, material, money and staff. While the organization may be robust it is also flexible and responsive to change.

Chaos theorists would say that the system has come to occupy a particular region of phase space. If this sounds a little too technical then let us substitute "space of all possible behaviors" for the term "phase space" and use the image of birds in the sky, or fish in a large lake. Individual fish can be located anywhere in the lake; they can be swimming in any direction and going at any speed. They can be coming to the surface for flies or grubbing along the bottom.

Imagine a space of many, many dimensions with axes indicating position, speed, direction, behavior and so on. Individual fish are represented by points in this "space of behaviors" and they can be dotted anywhere around this space.

Now think of a shoal of fish, or for that matter a flock of birds. This time the fish are close together in one region of the lake. They are all moving in one direction and going at the same speed. Instead of random points in our space of behaviors we now have all the points in a confined region—representing the collective behavior of the shoal, or the flock of birds.

To return to organizations. A rigid organization occupies a confined region of the space of behaviors. It is held there by a fixed "attractor"—the sets of rules, procedures and hierarchical structures imposed from above or from outside. By contrast, a self-organized system has generated its own "strange-attractor", one which keeps it confined within a given region of the space of behaviors—a little like the pattern which iron filings make on a piece of paper when a magnet is placed beneath. The strange attractor also allows a level of flexibility so that the boundaries to this space are adaptable. In other words the self-organized system can adjust to shifts in the external environment, or marketplace.

But what if those external changes are very sudden or very large. What happens, for example if we fire a shotgun into the air? The flock of birds will suddenly break apart, the birds flying away in all different directions. In place of a confined region within the space of behavior we suddenly have the entire space filled with birds flying in different directions and at different speeds. But after a short interval of time the birds come back together in some other region of the sky and begin to fly as a flock again. What has happened is that a pattern in a limited region of behavior space has broken down to fill all the space, then reorganized into a new pattern in some other region.

This is exactly what happens in "creative suspension". The existing organization begins to break down, old feedback loops are abandoned and new ones temporarily created; individuals and parts of the organization explore many other possibilities; new and different behaviors are tested out. In other words, the space of all possible actions is opened up and the organization allows itself a creative breathing space before self-organizing again. After this has happened the organization is again occupying a region of the behavior space but one that will be different from that which it originally occupied. The change may only be small, or it may be large-scale, but it has arisen from a degree of openness to different possibilities and opportunities, and the inherent creativity within the organization.

Scientific revolutions

This is similar to the argument advanced by the philosopher of science, Thomas Kuhn, in his book *The Structure of Scientific Revolutions*.[2] What he terms "normal science" is the everyday activity whereby scientific theories develop over the years. As new evidence is gathered an existing theory becomes modified, or replaced by a better theory. This process could continue for tens of years or even centuries, but underlying the whole approach is a particular way of seeing the world that remains unchanged in spite of specific theories being modified from time to time. In the case of the Ptolemaic system, for example, the earth was viewed as the centre of the universe with the sun, moon, planets and stars revolving in circular orbits around a fixed earth. As more accurate astronomical observations were gathered it became clear that circular orbits for the planets were not sufficient and the approach had to be modified using circles within circles. Things could have gone on indefinitely in this way, with corrections being added to corrections until Copernicus suggested a major paradigm shift—it is the sun that is at the centre, not the earth. Suddenly the whole pack of cards collapsed to be replaced by something totally different.

Likewise, with quantum theory, the Newtonian vision of the world as mechanism disappeared and was replaced by a more holistic, even organic approach.

In his book, *The Act of Creation*,[3] Arthur Koestler suggested that a scientific revolution is born when old structures totally break down and give rise to a period of "creative confusion". It is out of this confusion that something completely new emerges. Likewise, I am suggesting that if organizations exercise "creative suspension" and thereby enter a temporary period of creative confusion, this would be the ground out of which something new can grow.

In my own experience something similar happens in writing, and I have talked to other writers who have related accounts. I continue with a piece of writing until at some point I encounter a barrier. Faced with this nothing really can be done. Maybe I feel uneasy about what I have written but cannot articulate what is wrong. Maybe I have no idea as to what the next step could be, or what it is I am supposed to say. It is at this point I suspend action. Generally I lie down on the bed, close my eyes and don't even think. Then, inevitably—for it never fails—something will pop into my mind. From somewhere, something is telling me exactly what I must write next. I never think that it is a product of my own effort or thought. It simply appears and shows me the direction I must take.

Maybe I could even hazard another metaphor, and that is the "dark night of the soul". Generally a spiritual experience arises out of some practice of enlightenment. In some cultures it may happen during prayer or a religious ceremony. In others, through dancing or communal song. It is a time where the soul is uplifted and a person feels a strong sense of unity with a numinous "something" beyond themselves. But there is another road, less travelled, and that is the *via negativa*. It is the road in which everything is stripped away until nothing is left. It is an approach in which no attachments remain. Meister Eckhart, for example, looked at each attribute of God and declared that it was a human projection. Gradually God was stripped away until nothing remained except a pure potential, the Godhead. Likewise, where everything has been lost or suspended there is a possibility that something new and transcendent could enter.

But to return to Gentle Action, the metaphors above suggest that in a similar way an organization or group could also die and be reborn. In its new form it becomes at least as flexible and sensitive as the situation it faces. Now, with the help of human creativity and the art of working with complex systems, it may be possible to perceive a complex system more clearly and model it within the organization. This new understanding would be the basis for a novel sort of action, one that harmonizes with nature and society, that does not desire to dominate and control but seeks balance and good order and is based on respect for nature and society.

Gentle Action explores images of new organizations and institutions that would be able to sustain this watchfulness. In place of relatively mechanical, hierarchical and rule-bound organizations there would exist something more organic in nature.

Latent inhibition

At this point an interesting analogy can be made between the behavior of an organization and the responses of an individual. Both humans and animals live in highly complex environments. In the case of humans we were first surrounded by all the complexities of the natural world then, with the dawn of the twentieth century it was a world supplemented with highways, air travel, rapid communications, computers and video games. It was a world that was going faster and faster and in which decisions could no longer be mulled over within the atmosphere of a talking circle but at the click of a mouse. If we leave ourselves open to the stimuli that bombard us at every moment of our waking life we would be totally overwhelmed and unable to function and so the brain has developed a coping mechanism called "latent inhibition" which acts to inhibit or filter out most of the messages we receive and process only those that are necessary to our survival at any given moment. In other words while some stimuli can be ignored we are required to give attention to others. Of course this is not a product of recent evolution but was required by the first hunter-gatherers as they learned to deal with a wide variety of clues in the environment around them. It is just that our environment today is much faster and more complex.

So, for most people there is an adequate level of inhibition to keep the bombarding stimuli of the environment at bay. There are, however, some individuals who experience what is known as "low latent inhibition". The result is that such people are flooded with stimuli to the point that they can experience pathologies such as schizophrenia. This phenomenon was studied in more depth by researchers at the Department of Psychology at the University of Toronto during the first years of this century.

They discovered that individuals who had high IQs in combination with reduced latent inhibition, exhibited great creativity rather than suffering pathologies. Indeed their creativity appeared to be tied to openness and extraversion. It also appears to shed light on the age-old paradox of why genius and madness seem so closely tied together. As the researchers suggest in their 2002 paper, suppose a person faces a situation in which his or her current plans are failing to produce the desired outcome—exactly the situation we have been discussing in the case of organizations.[4] Low inhibition allows something novel or anomalous to emerge and permits a potentially promising new avenue of exploration to be opened up. Moreover the stress associated with an intractable situation acts to decrease latent inhibition and opens up the individual to gather new information when, as they put it, "nothing but categorical certainty once existed".

The analogy with the organization is clear. If it is over rigid, and with high levels of inhibition in processing incoming information about the marketplace, environment or surrounding social structure, then its plans, responses and strategies will be fixed. But if in some way it could open itself up to a wider world, to bring in factors that are unexpected and unusual; if it were more extraverted and better able to make unexpected interconnections then it should be possible to act in a far more creative way. Just as stress in the face of an intractable problem can lower inhibition in an individual so the organizational stress created by "creative suspension" can open that organization to new possibilities and new modes of behavior.

The University of Toronto researchers also make an analogy between natural selection and the creativity associated with reduced inhibition. Natural mutations occur during evolution and most of these are harmful or fatal and are therefore selected out. A small percentage, however, provide an advantage to the species and are propagated into future generations. Likewise low levels of inhibition allow for alternative modes of perception and cognition to be applied to a given situation. Most of these will be counterproductive and hence rejected or "culled", while the successes will be selected and implemented. This is the mark of a highly creative individual. But those who do not possess high intelligence, along with other advantageous personality traits, may be overpowered by the alternatives and even act on pathological ideas. Hence what can be the advantage of genius to some can lead to madness in others. The evolutionary metaphor could also be applied to organizations.

Under conditions of stress, when, for example, a tried and true strategy no longer works, the brain may reduce its "latent inhibitions" and allow more stimuli to be registered. What applies to an individual could equally apply to an organization as well, causing it to explore new and even unexpected solutions.

So what happens when there is a major change in an organization's external environment, a social crisis, environmental threat, upheaval in the marketplace, falling sales? The result will be a sense of stress to the organization. It then has four ways in which to respond:

a) If it is an over-rigid organization it can remain tied to its mission statement and policy documents and continue to behave as it has always behaved—even if that behavior is no longer producing satisfactory results.

b) It may simply be paralysed by the enormity and complexity of what it faces.

c) It can reduce its "latent inhibitions" and expose itself to all the complex issues that surround it. But if it lacks inherent creativity and has been unable to reorganize correctly it will simply jump from one strategy to the next and in essence sacrifice its ability to act in new and appropriate ways.

d) By exercising "creative suspension" the organization is exposed to considerable stress that allows for a flood of information about the environment in which it operates. But now, with sufficient creativity and intelligence, it can adopt new, appropriate and possibly even unanticipated strategies. The creative organization is able to respond to new situations in sustainable ways.

New dynamics

When organizations have exercised "creative suspension" something new may come into existence. With increased flexibility, they will now be able to internalize and model the complex dynamics of the systems that surround them. Rather than seeking to predict and control, they will be able to enter the flux of change and engage in those actions that are appropriate to each new situation.

Successful organizations of the future will have more open and organic structures. Their systems of communication will be closer to those of neural nets than to fixed telephone networks. (Neural nets involve pathways and nodes of connection with the ability to change their structure as the nature of the flow of information changes.) They will draw naturally upon the creativity of their employees and, in turn, employees will be self-directed and more satisfied by the exercise of their natural creativity and initiative within a caring environment.

But this does not mean that organizations will abandon leaders and managers. People with flair and the ability to make rapid decisions, who inspire confidence and exercise knowledge, intuition and creativity, will always be needed. Rather, the dominant stance, the artificially enhanced status, and the negativity associated with the notion of authority will change. New forms of leadership will respect the initiative and autonomy of others so that each person brings their best abilities to a particular task. In an emergency, for example, a natural leader will often come forward, yet as soon as the crisis is over that person will go back to carrying out their former tasks. Some management experts refer to this as "sapiential authority".[5]

In traditional and indigenous societies, leaders are elected in response to specific tasks and crises. Their authority does not arise by virtue of a particular fixed position that could be filled by a cipher. Rather individuals are chosen to give leadership during a specific emergency, or in order to carry out a given mission, and their authority arises from the confidence that is placed in them by the group. When that mission has been accomplished or that task ended, the "leader" returns to being just one more member of the group.

In a similar way, leaders will always be needed and be called upon in the new organizations. And as the particular challenge of a given situation changes, so too the internal structure of the organization will transform and particular individuals will be free to adopt new roles. As a result enhanced and more effective communications will take place in these new organizations.

Tacit knowledge

I am suggesting that when an organization engages in creative suspension this will allow its own natural creativity, and the skills of its employees to come to the fore. One of the most valuable things that an employee can bring is what is termed "tacit knowledge". Generally we think of knowledge as something we get out of a book, or download from the Internet. It may be a set of historical dates, a diagram of the engine of a car, a list of irregular French verbs, or the way to do long division. It is something that can be codified and learned. Tacit knowledge is something different. It is, for example, the knowledge of how to ride a bicycle. Could you explain to someone exactly how to ride a bicycle—the set of rules you must use to dispose your body? No, you simply get on a bike as a child, your parent runs beside you holding on to the back of the seat and at some point lets go and...what do you know, you are riding! Get on a bike twenty years later and you still possess that same tacit knowledge.

The name of the recipe book used in our village of Pari is *Dosi* (measures), and that is exactly what it contains—doses or measures. Look inside and the recipe for the cakes sold at the *sagra* (our September festival) is simply a list of ingredients and weights required. When she first saw this book, my daughter exclaimed, "But it doesn't tell you how to make the cake and how hot the oven should be." "But that is the *pratica*," came the reply, "You can't learn that from a book."

And so, for the local women, cooking involves tacit knowledge. Making a cake is a mixture of rules and flexibility. The fixed rules are found in the book, they govern the quantities of each ingredient required. Where skill and flexibility come in is in knowing how long to stir the mixture, understanding the temperature of a wood-fired oven without the use of a thermometer, and the exact moment when a cake is done.

The notion of tacit knowledge was explored by the philosopher of science, Michael Polanyi,[6] and his use of the term implies a silent or hidden knowledge. It is hidden because while we may know something— how to ride a bike, or cook a dish that is far superior to anyone else's—we don't actually know how we know this. After all, the best way to put a golfer off his or her game is to ask them, "Tell me exactly how you make that stroke. At what point do you cock your wrists?" The invitation to make that tacit knowledge explicit will totally put the player off their stroke for the rest of the game.

Clearly members of an organization have a wide variety of tacit knowledge and some of it is vitally important. And, while it is possible to formally evaluate explicit knowledge—this is the basis on which university degrees and diplomas are issued—it is far more difficult to put a price on tacit knowledge. I remember the managing director of one of Britain's largest chain of retail stores once telling me that all the members of his board except himself had MBAs, then adding "But I know how to sell underwear from a market stall".

It also could be the other way round. It may not be the CEO but a lowly worker who possesses a key piece of tacit knowledge. It may be his or her tacit knowledge, which when set side by side with the tacit knowledge of others, keeps a factory running, or a business in operation. I remember my experience several years ago trying to extract a cheque from a company. I went to their head office and then to the accounts department. At each step I was told how incredibly difficult it would be to issue the cheque, how it could take months, how many forms I would need to fill out. Finally, in the basement I found a man in a tiny office with a computer. He asked me what was worrying me. I explained. He took my name, tapped a few keys on the computer, looked up and said, "There, it's done. I've issued your cheque."

Dialogue

Let us look at suspension from yet another angle and that is the "Dialogue Process", as developed by the physicist, David Bohm.[7] In Bohm's approach a group of thirty to forty persons meet with no leader or program. The group comes together on a regular basis in order to build up trust. It does not have a specific topic for discussion, or goal and aim, but simply deals with whatever comes up during the dialogue itself. Bohm held that all of us hold onto some fixed nonnegotiable positions. For example, a person may believe in a woman's inalienable right to choose an abortion. Another may believe that all life is sacred and that abortion is never justified. When two people holding such opposing views meet, they have the choice of either avoiding the topic altogether, or starting to argue to the point where communication breaks down between them. However, in a dialogue circle there will always be people who occupy intermediary positions and who do not hold strongly to either of those two fixed positions. Such people can act to moderate the discussion.

That term "moderator" is also used to refer to a substance employed in a nuclear reactor. When fission of uranium occurs neutrons—elementary particles with zero electrical charge—are released. If those neutrons hit the nucleus of another uranium atom they can cause it to split. However, because they have no electrical charge—i.e. they are not attracted or repelled by other charged particles—the neutrons tend to fly away and escape from the reactor. The key is to slow them down by means of a series of collisions—using heavy water or graphite, for example. These substances are called moderators. They slow down the neutrons, keeping them inside the reactor where they will be able to hit other uranium nuclei and so allow the nuclear chain reaction to continue in a controlled way.

Likewise, when someone in the group becomes emotionally heated, because some remark has been made, or a deeply held position attacked, the others in the group will act as moderators, since they do not have a deep emotional investment in that particular position. The idea is not to persuade that person to change his or her belief, but rather to allow everything to slow down. In other words, to allow them to suspend their normal reactions for a moment. In so doing that person begins to become aware of just what is operating inside them. They start to realize how a particular word is triggering an emotional response, or the way in which a particular idea has been structured within both their mind and their body.

In this way a form of "creative suspension" becomes possible within the group as members begin to gain a deeper understanding of how they operate and what triggers their responses. As this happens, members of the group become less rigid and more creative and flexible in their responses. Bohm believed that this group can operate as a microcosm of the wider society outside, and by becoming more aware of the internal nature of our fixed positions, we can likewise make a creative change in society at large.

In this respect one could also draw upon the Native American process of arrival at consensus through the flow of active meaning around the traditional talking circle. This flow of meaning differs in its inherent dynamics from the conventional approach in which formal agreement is reached through discussion, argument and compromise. Rather than a fixed decision being drawn up and circulated at the end of a meeting, each person leaves the discussion knowing what he or she must do—even if circumstances should happen to change in the meantime. Likewise new organizations will therefore place their emphasis upon flexibility, creativity, intelligence and the ability to meet an unending challenge of change.

One could also make an analogy with architecture. In the traditional approach, an architect designs a building to be fit for a certain purpose. But over time the organization that commissioned that building may move and the structure may be occupied by other businesses with quite different functions. Therefore a newer generation of architects suggests that it is better to make buildings that can evolve and adapt to new situations. Similarly, organizations themselves can evolve. The idea of a "learning organization" and of "creative learning" has been proposed by a variety of experts, including Peter Senge.[8] Likewise Joseph Jaworski[9] stresses that true leadership has nothing to do with ordering people around but about enabling others to realize their human potential and break free of self-imposed limits.

The time is right

Another sensitivity that may go along with creative suspension is a deeper comprehension of when it is the correct time to move into action. One of the earlier activities of the Fetzer Institute had been to fund gatherings of Native American Elders and Western scientists. At the first meeting several of the Elders said that they would be performing a pipe ceremony early the following morning. On time the Western scientists assembled beside the lake on the property, but the Elders were nowhere to be seen. A couple of hours later they arrived to carry out the ceremony. When asked why they were late we were told "The time was not right. We can only do this ceremony when the time is right". This is something I have heard many times from Native Americans, that time has a certain quality and one should pause and suspend action until "the time is right".

To most of us, time has a mechanical quality. It is something recorded by a clock and reduced to numbers, and most of us are slaves to that mechanical time. Yet in a medieval village such as Pari where I now live, time is very much determined by the seasons and the sun. People go to work in the fields at first light and return when it is too hot to work, going out again in late afternoon. And so the period of work varies between spring, summer and winter. Even phases of the moon are important. Parsley, for example, must only be sown with the moon is full in spring.

There is even a similar sense to that of Native America of the time being "right". Our festivals in August and September attract large crowds who come to eat and dance, and so tables and benches must first be erected in the two piazzas of the village. This requires a great deal of preparation on the morning of the event, but no one posts a notice saying at what time of day the task must be done. Men just appear in the square, arriving from different directions, all more or less at the same time, as if they sense that the time is now "right" to work together.

Individuals in suspension

One of the most remarkable recent examples of creative suspension is that exercised by Natascha Kampusch,[10] an Austrian girl who was kidnapped at the age of ten by Wolfgang Priklopil and kept in a basement for eight years. Even though a child, Natascha felt that she was inherently stronger than her captor, and that as she grew older she would also become physically stronger and eventually would be able to break free. On the other hand, she was troubled by his threat that, should she escape, he would go on a killing spree.

She recalls that after two years of captivity, "I made a deal with myself that the Natascha of the future would come back to free that little 12-year-old girl". A truly outstanding example of wisdom and maturity, in that while she felt unable to take a positive action at that particular time in her life, she knew that by allowing herself to grow in maturity the time would eventually come when she could take the appropriate action and free herself. After her escape Priklopil committed suicide.

The late British composer, Sir Michael Tippett, has spoken of "holding" the music inside himself until it was ready to be written down.[11] There would be a long period before composition began, and then the music would begin to appear to him. The music was in some sense invoked, yet with no forceful act of will involved. In some ways it was closer to a sense of "possession". It was as if Tippett were being invaded by the music. But that music, inside the body, needed to be sung or performed and therefore it generated a tension within his body to the point where Tippett became ill. As he put it, the body "gets tired of being the endless servant of something."

As with Tippett, so too the sculptor Anish Kapoor[12] has spoken of "holding the intention" with his own work. Unlike some sculptors, and particularly in his earlier work, Kapoor does not generally begin with a series of drawings, or macquettes, which are then developed into full-sized works. Rather he holds an intention and allows the work to grow. Obviously he has a physical involvement in the process in terms of carving, or adding, but it would be as though the sculpture begins to grow in an organic way, rather than a clear vision being imposed on the piece of stone, for example. In this one could recall Michelangelo's remark that the sculpture already existed in the stone, all he had to do was chip away what was not needed until the inner form revealed itself.

I had a similar experience of "holding" when I first moved from Canada to the village of Pari in 1994. My wife and I arrived with just two suitcases and the intention of returning to Canada after spending three months in Italy and three in London. Over the next weeks in Pari

I went for walks, or simply sat in a deck chair in the sun. I had no books with me, which was particularly unusual. In fact, I did nothing for three months. People have often asked me what I did during that period. When I reply "Nothing" they say, "Sure, but did you get a lot of writing done? Did you do some research? Did you come up with an idea for the next book". "No", I would reply, "I did nothing."

Most people found that impossible to believe, because I am generally a very active person working on several things at once. But I truly did nothing during that period. Yet at the end, when I moved to London, I entered into a highly creative period and began work on several new books. Maybe deep down a part of me knew that I had to suspend activity. Maybe in some unconscious way I had even subtly arranged all the web of accidental circumstances that caused me to end up for three months in a medieval village in Italy, rather than carrying out my original intention to move directly to London from Canada.

The Fetzer Institute: Organizational suspension

It is one thing for an individual to exercise a creative suspension but quite another for a large organization to actually suspend its activities. However this is exactly what happened a few years ago at the Fetzer Institute in the United States. Its founder, John E. Fetzer, began his career as an electrical engineer and ended up with a radio and television empire that allowed him to purchase the Detroit Tigers baseball team. But, in addition to business, he had an interest in what he called the "unseen elements" in life, and was concerned with the integration of body, mind and spirit. To this end he created the Fetzer Foundation in Kalamazoo, Michigan. John Fetzer died in 1991 but the Institute, with its $400 million endowment, continued to flourish.

Under its President, Robert F. Lehman, the Fetzer Foundation underwent its first transformation into the Fetzer Institute and moved from being a funding body to beginning to promote research and work that engaged in the connection between the inner and outer life. The new Institute also began to create Fetzer Fellows and ran a number of meetings and conferences on their grounds including a circle of Western Scientists and Native American Elders. But then Lehman was forced to retire due to ill health and the Institute went through an intermediary period.

It was then, in March of 2002, that the organization decided to enter into a period of "creative suspension". By focussing on what happened over the next years we begin to gain a clearer understanding of just what creative suspension means. Much of what I have learned of the Fetzer experience comes from speaking with their President, Tom Beech, who first became involved with the organization in September of that year and was officially made president on February 1, 2003.

As Beech emphasized, Creative Suspension did not mean doing nothing but rather involved a very active process that highlighted a special quality of listening. While it was certainly true that work did not go ahead on some projects the emphasis was not so much on the suspension of all activities but on the suspension of judgment to the point where people could become open to a new and deeper way of listening, both within the organization and to what was occurring outside, including those with past associations to Fetzer and the Fetzer Fellows. In the months and then years that followed each individual looked at what had formed the organization and examined all their assumptions about principles and values. This was not always easy. For some people the future looked so unclear that they became frightened and frustrated. Some asked, "What on earth is going on?" Others wondered what exactly was their place. And so there were periods of impatience and of creative confusion but the organization also realized that it was necessary to enter into "the dark night of the soul" and to do so each person had to be accountable and in their hearts hold onto the process they were exploring. In that way they were able to "come out the other side".

In this book we have explored the tacit knowledge that each individual carries within themselves. Fetzer's suspension also revealed what was of key importance; that everyone from the most senior official to those responsible for catering, care of the grounds and guest services had a deep sense of caring—"we treat people and the building with love". So that those who visited the Institute felt looked after and better able to engage in their work.

This process of suspension continued until at some point what could perhaps be called the founding principles began to resurface in a new and creative way. What is more, the nature of the organizational structure began to change from that of a more traditional form into something fresher and more creative. Where other organizations have their mission statement and inner hierarchical structure—which is often echoed in the physical structure of the building itself, the Fetzer Institute began to see itself as a series of interpenetrating rings that included its various partners and advisors who were all deeply engaged. Along with that new form of organization emerged a fresh vision, fostering "the awareness of the power of love and forgiveness".

Rob Lehman, who was now the chairman of the board of advisors had often referred to what he called "the common work" but now the

Fetzer Institute realized that it was just one player in a much larger constellation. The result is that each member of the organization from groundsperson to president is able to understand their new direction in greater depth. The lessons were

• Learning how to communicate

• Listening

• Learning that working relationships must always be based on trust

For Tom Beech, the president, creative suspension has become something like that "little silence" that happens when a person stops talking and begins to listen.[13]

✄ Reflections on Chapter 5

1. Think about the significant difference between an act of creative suspension and "just doing nothing".

2. Clearly there are times when it is necessary to act quickly and there are times when a temporary suspension may be necessary. Try to find examples of the two and define what is different about them.

3. How clearly do you see a social, economic or environmental situation? Do you have a sense of subtle internal biases? Do you feel influenced by media and those around you?

4. Think of your own life. Where does your valuable tacit knowledge lie and how do you exercise it?

5. Look at your work or a social group of which you are a member. What role does leadership play and how effective is it?

6. What do you think would happen if your group or business were to enter into an act of creative suspension?

7. Are your judgments made though emotional reactions or by carefully adding up all the pros and cons? (In this respect it may be useful to recall that Carl Jung wrote that we exercise two "rational functions" to judge a situation. One is "thinking" and the other "feeling". Some people are balanced and use both thinking and feeling in a situation. You can discover where you lie on the scale by taking one of the many on-line tests based on the Myers Briggs approach. See for example, http://www. humanmetrics.com/cgi-win/JTypes2.asp

Notes

1. I first proposed the notion of Creative Suspension in *Creativity Research Journal* 1, 131, (1989).

2. Thomas Kuhn, *The Structure of Scientific Revolutions* (Chicago: University of Chicago Press, 3rd edition, 1996).

3. Arthur Koestler, *The Act of Creation* (London: Hutchinson, 1964).

4. Jordan B. Peterson, Kathleen W. Smith and Shelly Carson, "Openness and extraversion are associated with reduced latent inhibition: replication and commentary." *Personality and Individual Differences* 33, (2002) 1137-1147.

5. Robert Theobald "sapiential authority" http://www.manage.gov.in/managelib/faculty/vksingh.htm. There are also articles on sapiential authority on http://www.blackwell-synergy.com.

6. Michael Polanyi, *The Tacit Dimension* (New York: Doubleday & Co., 1966).

7. David Bohm, *On Dialogue* (London: Routledge, 1996).

8. Peter Senge, *The Fifth Discipline: The art and practice of the learning organization* (New York: Doubleday Business, 2006).

9. Joseph Jaworski, *Synchronicity: The inner path of leadership* (San Francisco: Berrett-Koehler, 1998).

10. Natascha Kampusch's story was carried in a variety of newspaper articles and television interviews. For a more recent overview see *The Independent*, August 10, 2007.

11. Tippett, discussion with the author.

12. Kapoor, discussion with the author.

13. A telephone interview with Tom Beech, September 14, 2007.

Chapter 6.
Trust and ethics

"Trust was shaken today. Credit depends on trust. If trust disappears, then credit disappears, and you have a systemic issue."

Thomas Mayer, chief European economist at Deutsche Bank in Frankfurt, (*New York Times,* August 10, 2007).

"...commerce dies the moment, and is sick in the degree, in which men cannot trust each other".

Henry Ward Beecher (1813-1887) US clergyman, abolitionist, *Webster's Electronic Quotebase*, ed. Keith Mohler, 1994.

There is one other factor that must be examined before we go on to explore examples of Gentle Action and that is the whole issue of trust. We have seen that an exercise in creative suspension may allow an organization to restructure in more open and flexible ways. But a key issue in such restructuring must be the return of trust. Trust, Ethics and Honesty are essential elements in any organization, workplace, community or individual life. Indeed a Gentle Action that does not embody these values would be somewhat empty. Therefore Gentle Action must be placed within the context of social and individual trust and we must discover just where trust stands in our lives today.

We all feel that people should judge us as being honest in our dealings, and hope that those around us are equally honest. It is also important to have ethical standards in our work and daily lives. We know that those in the medical profession, for example, must at times make very difficult decisions and in such cases they are helped by ethics committees, as well as the ethical standards established by their professional organizations. Ethical standards are also important in deciding what sort of medical and biological research should be allowed, and what should come under scrutiny. We would also hope that ethical standards are upheld by law firms, accountants and a host of other professions.

Sometimes the issue of ethics is associated with a particular religion as, for example, with the European Baha'i Business Forum, and the Jewish Association for Business Ethics in the UK. But there are also those who do not adhere to any religious belief system yet would consider themselves to be bound by strong ethical standards in all their dealings. (An interesting debate between the writer Umberto Eco and Cardinal Martini of Milan, on how an agnostic would construct a set of ethical values can be found in their book *Belief and Unbelief*.[1])

Trust is also of great importance in daily life; it is the glue that holds society together, alive and functional. Without trust, our institutions would collapse. Confucius argued that weapons, food and trust are essential to government, and if a ruler can't hold on to all three then he should first give up weapons, then food, but trust must be guarded to the end.

But just how healthy is trust within our modern world, and particularly within North America and Europe? We certainly read and hear a great deal about the current "crisis in trust". And the rise of the celebrity as a major figure in large-scale fundraising is based upon the observation that the public places more trust in a pop star than they do in a politician. Some commentators are unhappy with what they see as the rise of a new sort of market environment, with a focus on short-term profits and short-term goals. The result, they say, is an emphasis on expediency, and an erosion of ethical standards. Within this climate of uncertainty there may be less trust in balance sheets and the company reports of major businesses. It was within that particular atmosphere that the accounting scandals of Enron and Arthur Andersen, the collapse of Barings Bank, and the price-fixing scandal at the auction houses of Sotheby's and Christie's came to light. At the time of writing, an employee of France's second-largest bank Société Genéralé has been charged with breach of trust, fabricating documents and illegally accessing computers in the biggest rogue trading scandal in investment banking history. The result was the loss of almost 5bn euros ($7bn) for the bank. The trader told investigators that his practices were widespread and that the banking hierarchy turns a blind eye as long as a profit is being made.[2]

There is also the issue of the growth of global electronic networks, which enable financial speculation to take place at the click of a mouse, the exploded dot-com bubble, the growing acceptance of the notion that "Greed is Good", the tide of MBA graduates making easy money in the markets, the tremendous influx of pension money and private investment into equities—all seeking to save in an easy and "assured" way for retirement. All this seems to indicate that trust is being compromised. And if it is, just how serious has the situation become? In the sections below we shall look at some examples in which trust in the institutions and organizations around us has become threatened.

Medicine and the law

Erosion of trust occurs in other areas of life. For example, there is concern within the medical profession of Britain and the United States that less trust is being put in doctors. A number of conferences have been held, and study papers commissioned, in order to discuss this crucial issue.

One example is the relationship of doctors and hospitals to drug companies. When a research paper on a drug evaluation is published in a refereed scientific journal one would hope that the researchers involved are impartial. But what if they work in a hospital that receives large funding from drug corporations? And what if the doctors themselves are receiving a grant from the very company whose drug they are evaluating?

Yet another issue is the inducements made to doctors to prescribe particular medications. An article in the *New York Times* of May 10, 2007, for example, drew attention to the increasing use of what are called "atypical antipsychotics" prescribed for children. These are powerful drugs, known to have undesirable side effects in some cases. Nevertheless their use is on the increase and, according to some, this is a direct result of financial incentives made by the manufacturers. (Minnesota is the only state in the US where public disclosure of such incentives is required.) Payments to doctors by manufacturers of these particular drugs rose six-fold during the period 2000-2005, to a total of $1.6 million. During that same period the use of antipsychotics rose nine-fold. Payments to individual doctors ranged from $51 to $689,000, with an average of $1,750. The doctors were being paid as consultants or for giving "public talks". Guidelines on the prescription of atypicals to children from a panel of doctors were published in the *Journal of the American Academy of Child and Adolescent Psychiatry*. Three of the four doctors on that panel served as speakers or consultants to the drug companies involved.

In the United Kingdom, the case of Harold Shipman, a doctor found guilty of killing at least 250 patients (and possibly many more), seriously shook the public's confidence in the profession, for this involved far more than the actions of one aberrant doctor. In the Shipman Enquiry Report for the UK Secretary of State for Health, Dame Janet Smith argued that if the General Medical Council had done its job properly, Shipman's serial murders would have been discovered and stopped decades earlier. The GMC, she wrote, despite the motto "Protecting Patients—Guiding Doctors" emblazoned on its letterhead, focused "too much on the interests of the doctors and not sufficiently on the protection of patients."[3] To take but one example: Shipman visited Mrs. Renate Overton, a 46-year-old patient with asthma, at her home and injected her with 20 mg of morphine. In this particular case the patient did not die immediately but went into an irreversible coma and was admitted to an intensive care unit where she later died. As its turned out, the senior physicians in charge of the ICU knew that Shipman had administered a lethal dose of a contraindicated drug, but never reported this or even questioned him.

More recently the media carried a story about a male nurse in a British hospital who was discovered to have been deliberately stopping patients' hearts because of the sense of power he derived from shocking them back to life again.[4] Again one wonders why the hospital authorities involved did not question the high incidence of such emergency procedures being used. Maybe it has something to do with the shadow side of trust. Doctors assume that members of their profession are always acting in the best interests of their patients, and simply do not wish to look at their behavior too closely, or question their ethics. In the preface to his play, *Doctor's Dilemma* George Bernard Shaw writes that a doctor would "allow a colleague to decimate a whole countryside" rather then violate the bond of professional etiquette by giving him away.

In a sense this whole issue of the abuse of trust exposes a particular paradox. Trust is essential for a society to function correctly and indeed most people will exercise trust in a spontaneous manner. Later in this chapter we shall meet the research of Paul Zak and others who had engaged in laboratory games in which randomly selected partners showed levels of trust in donating sums of money to each other. However within his sample were just a few people who sought only personal gain and did not donate back to people who had been generous to them. In other words the whole issue of trust is a difficult one because it suggests that within most of our interactions we can indeed assume that those around us will operate in an atmosphere of trust, however there are also those occasional individuals who do not appear to be touched by the virtue of trust.

In an earlier chapter we learned how standards of cleanliness and daily practice in British hospitals have declined to such an extent that they are dangerous places in which to be ill. This is yet another reason why people may exercise a measure of distrust of hospitals, and the various social organizations that surround them. In addition, a friend who has spent many years in the medical profession recently told me that it is her experience that patients in the US with serious diagnoses are now seeking second and third opinions. This was not, she felt, because they questioned the competence of their first doctor, but rather because they knew that doctors today are overworked and distracted, and may not be able to give full attention to a person's medical records.

To move to another profession, a friend who had practised all his life as a lawyer spoke of the time when he could telephone the opposing lawyer and discuss the case, knowing that his adversary would never take advantage of what they discussed together. But today he felt he would be unable to trust the word of a "young hotshot lawyer" so that all matters dealing with a case would have to be set down on paper.

Trust in science

The role of trust in science has a long history. When Britain's Royal Society was founded in 1660 it was firmly based on the notion of trust, and that the reports sent in by Fellows would be trustworthy and experimentally transparent. The society even set out rules whereby papers submitted to its *Philosophical Transactions* should explain how particular experiments were carried out so that others could reproduce them.[5]

Indeed surveys show that science is the most trusted profession. It is generally assumed that scientific results can be trusted, and that scientists will always tell the truth about their work. Most scientific journals operate under what is called a "referee" system, in which each paper submitted is sent to one or two referees, experts in that particular field, for review. The referee is expected to assess the scientific merits of the paper and suggest any changes or clarifications. But in the main, where experimental results are reported, the referee assumes that these are a true report of what was observed and measured. Nevertheless, from time to time fraud does enter into science and therefore compromises our whole level of trust in what has become one of the most important enterprises in the modern world.

We learned earlier of Sir Cyril Burt's fraudulent results on the relationship of IQ to inherited intelligence. It is one of those rare cases in which an individual scientist is so convinced about the truth of some new theory or effect that he or she "massages" data in order to make a more convincing argument. This is probably not done with any aim of career promotion or self-advancement, rather it is when those few scientists feel so passionately about the truth of their ideas that they need to convince more skeptical colleagues.

(Having worked in a laboratory environment as a young scientist I have witnessed cases in which sets of data were rejected because they did not back up the hypothesis that the individual scientist was attempting to demonstrate. This was generally accompanied by a level of somewhat embarrassed self-justification such as "the solution may have been contaminated" or "this instrument probably needs recalibrating".)

The more pernicious situation occurs when there is a great deal of money and investment involved in particular results, so that enormous pressure is placed on ordinary career scientists working for a large company. It may involve the development of a new drug, or the correlation between smoking and cancer, or addiction to nicotine, or the safety of GM crops or pesticides. In such cases the problem may be less about manipulating data than omitting certain results from a report. For this reason, fraud is more likely to occur in the biomedical field than in physics or chemistry.

So how healthy is trust in science? A panel of experts commissioned by the European Union said that they "must continue to address the issue of trust and legitimacy of science and technology in Europe".[6] In 2002 the Royal Society ran a national forum entitled "Do we trust today's scientists?" and suggested that sets of ethical guidelines be established for scientific research. In addition "trust was viewed as pivotal to effectively mediating the relationship between science and society."[7] In 2000 an inquiry by the British House of Lords concluded that "society's relationship with science is in a critical phase". Trust had been rocked by the outbreak of BSE, commonly known as mad cow disease, and by widespread suspicion and unease about the rapid progress of biotechnology. It went on: "Our recommendation is clear: a new culture of effective public dialogue and openness. We believe we are 'pushing with the pile of the carpet' on this." Moreover, there was a tendency for scientists to be patronizing when they spoke of "the public understanding of science". "Scientists are servants of society, not its masters," said the report, "and people should be properly informed about what we scientists are doing."[8]

The Canadian Centre for Ethics in Public Affairs (in 2005) pointed to a certain irony, that while polls in the US, Canada and Europe indicated that scientists came out top when it came to trust, and were viewed as the objective pursuers of truth, on the other hand politicians and business leaders were mistrusted. But, the Centre, argued, "scientific knowledge and its applications (such as medicine) cannot be treated as though independent from industry and government". Therefore "what emerges from the 'trusted' space of the scientific laboratory into our daily lives through government policies or consumer products and technologies may not deserve the levels of trust we have invested in science and its institutions. It is time to reexamine just what it means for Canadians to 'trust in science.' "[9]

An interesting sociological sideline on the issue of trust in science surfaced during the early days of the "cold fusion" debate, sparked off by claims, in 1989, from Stanley Pons and Martin Fleischmann at the

University of Utah, and Steven Jones at Brigham Young University, that they had produced nuclear fusion at room temperature.[10] In the initial weeks following the announcements, the scientific debate became very heated and much of it was conducted via the Internet rather than through the normal refereed scientific journals where the delay between submission of a paper and its final publication can be many months. While the proposition that nuclear fusion was taking place in a liquid initially appeared implausible, it was only a matter of weeks, or even days, before theoretical physicists were able to suggest possible mechanisms whereby it could occur—if indeed it had. More subtle was the whole issue of trust. Experimental results coming out of the Ivy League universities or, say, the University of California, are well trusted—the scientists involved could be relied upon. But what level of trust could there be to controversial results that came from universities in the state of Utah? Added to this were the vested interests in their long investment in hot fusion research from such organizations as the Princeton Plasma Physics Laboratory.

That same year I attended a meeting of the American Physical Society during which cold fusion was discussed. After that particular session, a group of East Coast physicists were talking at the next table. They were expressing their total lack of trust in the results that had been presented and felt it important that the scientists involved be discredited. In fact the issue was as much about levels of trust in science, as about reproducing experimental findings. Later a similar debate arose around the notion that "memories" could be stored in water, a proposal that would provide a theoretical basis for homeopathy.

An even more shocking example occurred in the 1950s when the Princeton University physicist, David Bohm, developed an alternative approach to quantum theory called "hidden variables". It was also the period in which Bohm appeared before the House Un-American Activities Committee, refused to name names and was arrested for contempt of Congress. Even though he was acquitted, the president of Princeton University forbade Bohm to set foot on the campus, and shortly after this Bohm left for Brazil. While he was in Brazil, J. Robert Oppenheimer called a seminar at Princeton to discuss Bohm's theory. One by one the physicists present denounced Bohm, not on scientific grounds but as being a "fellow traveller," "a Trotskyite" "a traitor" and "a public nuisance". And when the assembled physicists were unable to find a flaw in Bohm's new theory, Oppenheimer suggested, "If we cannot disprove Bohm, then we must agree to ignore him".[11]

Word quickly went out and years later I met distinguished physicists who would still tell me that Bohm's theory was wrong. When I asked them to explain where the error lay, the reply would be along the lines of, "I've never actually read Bohm's paper, but I don't have to, I just know that it's wrong".

We should therefore remember that scientists are first and foremost human beings with all the weaknesses, ambitions and capacity for deception of other human beings. They may have entered their profession because they had a deep desire to search for the truth of the natural world. The vast majority of them keep to the highest professional standards, since creativity and discovery are themselves much greater rewards than money. Nevertheless, a few of them become seduced into cutting corners, or omitting results that could compromise their theories or their employers, if not on rare occasions falsifying results.

And what about the universities that produce these scientists and other experts? They are having to contend with a phenomenon sometimes nicknamed "the creep" (in the sense of something that moves slowly so that at first we may not notice the effect). Suppose a wealthy man sends his son to a top university in the United States. The young man may not have worked that hard and therefore is in danger of failing, or at least of getting only the lowest grades. However, the faculty will be willing to raise his grades because they fear the dean's reaction if the father phones the university and complains. In addition, if the percentage of A and A– grades are seen to fall in a particular University, its graduate school may look less attractive.

(In fact "the creep" may not be that new. When I started my own university teaching a student had been failed by my predecessor because his examination results were simply too poor for a pass. I was called in by the head of department and asked to take a second look at his exam paper because he was "a decent young man". I did look again and agreed that, while I could add an odd mark or two, it would still not be enough for a pass. At this the department head said, "I don't think you are hearing me. This young man crews on my yacht. I need him around next year.")

This issue of "the creep" should be set in the wider context of the way universities are operating today. Traditionally they were the transmitters of culture, learning and independent thought. They fostered scholarship, original research and critical thinking. Its members acted as arbiters who accredited knowledge. But today's universities are producing knowledge in a "hothouse" atmosphere, one that is characterized more by the corporation than the campus. They are increasingly influenced by financial and institutional pressures, for their financial and administrative sides have passed into the hands of those who act like CEOs; individuals who appear to be thinking in terms of "the bottom line" and short-term results that will satisfy corporate sponsors and government funding. As a result, universities are in danger of becoming no more than "knowledge factories"; a source of human capital in the form of highly skilled workers.

Subjects taught in universities are often not chosen because of their intrinsic importance, but on the grounds that they will qualify students for future work. Subjects that may not be attractive to potential employers are now dropped as being "orchid disciplines". In 2003, for example, the British Education Secretary, Charles Clarke, speaking at University College Worcester, said, "I don't mind there being some medievalists around for ornamental purposes, but this is no reason for the state to pay for them". He went on to declare that the state should only fund subjects of "clear usefulness".[12]

(I should point out that while I must take responsibility for the ideas and proposals made in this book, the above excursion on the present role of universities were the conclusions of a conference "The Future of the Academy" held at the Pari Center in September 2000.)[13]

Bobby on the beat

The British police force had its origins in the cabinet minister, Robert Peel's sponsoring of the Metropolitan Police Act of 1829 which created a uniformed police force whose task would be to prevent crime through conspicuous patrolling. Each "bobby" (named for Robert Peel) had a particular "manor", a small area of London that he patrolled on foot. The police manual of the period indicated "he should be able to see every part of his beat at least once in ten minutes or a quarter of an hour". Police were to be impersonal and patient, and their authority was to come not only from the crown but also from the cooperation of the citizenry.

A constable knew the people in his "manor" and would stop to talk and anticipate any problems that might arise. When a young person got into trouble there would be a strict paternal "talking-to", and the constable would continue to keep an eye on the potential offender. In turn, the public placed great trust in the local bobby and would keep him informed of any concerns they had, or what they felt to be suspicious characters or actions. In this way policing was mainly preventative and became a form of Gentle Action that arose out of the mutual trust of the public and the police force.[14]

This practice then spread to the rest of England and its ethos was typified in the long running television series *Dixon of Dock Green* that began in 1955. In each program the genial, if somewhat paternalistic,

George Dixon would greet his audience with a salute and an "Evening all", then a little homily, or something to the effect that "all's quiet on the manor tonight". The episode would then follow Dixon in giving assistance to an elderly person, dealing with a difficult spouse, or talking to a cheeky young boy. What crime there was amounted to petty larceny and the greatest sin for Dixon was the remote possibility of corruption in the police force, "There's nothing worse than a bent copper".

But beat policing is extremely labour-intensive, and it was soon judged an impractical way to provide full coverage of an area. The system was replaced by randomly moving police cars that were supposed both to reassure the public and intercept crimes in progress. Yet at the same time trust in the police began to wane. Britain was becoming a multiracial country and social and economic tensions were on the rise. This made for a dangerous powder keg just waiting to be lit, and the result was very serious rioting by youths in South London in 1981. It involved a large number of injuries, and with some members of the public protesting that the police had acted in ways that were brutal and unjust. The official report by Lord Scarman indicated that police had become too remote from their communities, and that local citizens should have more input into police policy-making. In short, trust was eroding in what had previously been an excellent system, and with that erosion effective policing had fallen from the successes of its initial goal.[15]

While trust in the British bobby may have suffered, in the main the British public retains a good degree of faith in their police. This is a far cry from the state of affairs in Northern Island where things became so bad that one section of the divided population had virtually zero trust in their police force, the Royal Ulster Constabulary.

For centuries there had been tensions in Northern Ireland. This resulted from the settlements and plantations that had been established by the British and involved the immigration of Protestant Scots into the indigenous Catholic area of Northern Ireland. Tensions were further created when senior positions in many areas of society were filled almost exclusively by Protestants. In particular, while the Royal Ulster Constabulary (RUC) did contain a few Catholic officers, it was mainly seen as a tool of Protestant interests.

The Catholic minority therefore placed no trust in the RUC, for they believed that it shielded criminals and failed to investigate fully when serious crimes were perpetrated against Catholics. This lack of trust became so serious that most Catholics would simply not have any dealings with the police, even if their cooperation could have been helpful.

For decades during the twentieth century the province saw extreme violence with murder perpetrated by both sides. Only in recent years has it seemed that true peace would be possible. And while trust is a very difficult social good to reestablish, it became severely tested by a report that appeared in January 2007. In this report the Police Ombudsman, Nuala O'Loan, indicated that evidence showed that during the 1990s there had been collusion between police and their informers. O'Loan upheld a complaint by the father of murdered Raymond McCord, Jr. that "over a number of years police acted in such a way as to protect informants from being fully accountable to the law." These informants had been responsible for the murders of 10 people; 10 attempted murders; 10 punishment shootings and 13 punishment attacks; a bomb attack in Monaghan; and 72 instances of other crimes, including 17 counts of drug dealing, criminal damage, extortion, and intimidation.

Other abuses by the police included informants being "babysat" during interviews, to avoid incriminating themselves, the creation of false interview notes, and the blocking of searches of potential arms dumps. What is more, the officers involved destroyed files in order to protect themselves from prosecution. The report also concluded that the officers involved "could not have operated as they did without the knowledge and support at the highest levels of the RUC and the PSNI." (In 2001 the RUC had been replaced by the Police Service of Northern Ireland [PSNI].)[16]

Trust or suspicion

The examples above are disheartening, and most of us would agree that in many areas of life trust is becoming compromised within our society. Yet not everyone takes that position, so maybe we should hear from the opposite side. After all, the examples given above could be turned in quite different directions. I have quoted them as examples of ways in which trust is being compromised but, on the other hand, the great sense of shock they produce could be taken as evidence that they are rare and distressing exceptions to a very general rule that trust continues to operate as a steady basis in our society. At least that would be the sort of argument advanced by philosophy professor, Onora O'Neill.

The 2002 BBC Reith Lectures were given by O'Neill, Principal of Newnham College, Cambridge and entitled "A Question of Trust".[17] (Note that by deliberately giving the name of her university I implicitly increase the level of trust the reader will afford to her argument—recall the difference in trust of Princeton University versus universities in

Utah!) O'Neill agrees that the general public perception indicates that our trust in institutions, businesses, public services, politicians, scientists, business people, accountants, auditors and even the medical profession has been treated with suspicion. Their word is doubted, their motives are questioned. Ironically, she remarks, the very journalists who write and broadcast about this issue happen to be members of the least trusted profession. (Or at least that was true when I began to write this chapter, but a recent survey in the UK indicated that politicians are now less trusted than journalists or real estate agents).

On the other hand, O'Neill argues, ordinary people, at least in the United Kingdom, continue to operate in their daily lives on the basis of trust in institutions and between individuals. It is her opinion that when one examines the actual way people behave, and the actions they take, then trust appears to operate at the same substantial level as it did in the past. Her feeling is that our current perception of the "erosion of trust" does not accord with our everyday actions. Indeed, for O'Neill it is not so much that trust is lacking today, but that we have engendered a culture of suspicion.

Trust in action

If O'Neill is correct, and I am not sure that she is, then let us look at some of the ways in which trust operates around us. When you walk into a bank, get onto a bus, order a book from Amazon, take out car insurance, or mail a cheque you are acting under the assumption that the associated social institutions can be trusted. Take that simple action of mailing a birthday card to a friend in another country. It is based on trust in an international postal service, on sorters, airlines, baggage handlers, customs officers and a service at the other end whereby the card will be delivered quickly and to the correct address. Our everyday postal system therefore runs on a vast network of trust, as do so many other organizations that function for us on a day-to-day basis.

Let us examine that example of the postal service in a little more detail. Rome had its *cursus publicus* in which mail was rapidly transported to all regions of the empire, and a series of inspections ensured a well functioning system. Even with the fall of the Roman Empire this system persisted into the 9th century. However, with the end of the Carolingian dynasty in Europe, a period of confusion resulted. In the political unrest that followed, highways were no longer kept in repair and the postal system declined. Without high levels of trust, such a complex system could not be maintained—in this we are reminded of the need for a strong web of feedback loops to maintain a self-organized system. It was only with the growth of commerce that the guilds began to develop a reliable postal system, such as the Butcher Post. By the 13th century the main commercial centres in Italy, as well as the Champagne area of northern France, were linked by a reliable postal service. There was even a service between Venice and Constantinople. By the late 15th century an international postal system had been reinstated with 20,000 couriers. Clearly a system of such complexity could only operate on the very strict basis of mutual trust.[18]

Another system that functions on trust is money. After all money of high denominations is no more than pieces of paper that are worth almost nothing in themselves. Once bank notes held a promissory sentence in which the US Treasury promised to pay the bearer the sum of "one dollar". That promise was dropped some time ago, without anyone particularly noticing the change, for the whole system essentially works on the basis of trust. There are even systems called "complementary currencies" that operate in some regions such as the city of Ithaca, New York. This consists of pieces of paper distributed by the community that can be redeemed for goods or services. Most people learning about complementary money are puzzled and ask, "But how can it work. The paper isn't worth anything". But in this it is no different from a euro or a dollar bill—it is based on a network of mutual trust and exchange.[19]

The children's Christmas film *Miracle on 34th Street* ends in a court case in which the State of New York asks a judge to rule that Santa Claus does not exist. Just before announcing his decision, the judge is handed a Christmas card by a little girl that contains a one-dollar bill. The words "In God we trust" are underlined on the bill. The judge rules that if the Federal Government places its trust in something that cannot be proved, then the State of New York is in no position to rule against Santa Claus. Possibly he could have added that every US citizen also places its trust in the exchangeability of a piece of paper, a dollar bill, that in itself has virtually no material value.

Complex systems such as a postal service and a national currency are very much like the self-organized systems we met in chapter three. In this case, trust is the name of the feedback loops involved and, as with other self-organized systems, one part of the system is nested within another. So clearly issues of trust cannot be isolated from the social contexts in which they operate. Why, for example, did New York City's crime rate drop during the 1990s, and the subway become a safer means of travel? A clue can be found in George L. Kelling and Catherine Coles' *Fixing Broken Windows: Restoring order and reducing crime in our communities*, which pointed out that a street filled with litter, or a building with broken windows, acts as a catalyst for further vandalism.[20] If society does not care about its streets and buildings, then disaffected members of the public very quickly pick up the subliminal message involved and cease to respect their environment. Kelling and Coles's argument was applied by David Gunn of the New York Transit Authority who first removed graffiti from subway trains, and then cracked down on fare dodging. Fare dodging may appear to be a rather minor thing compared with a violent mugging, but Gunn believed that ignoring fare dodgers and running coaches filled with graffiti created an environment in which more serious crime could flourish.

We have already learned of the work accomplished by Claire and Gordon Shippey in their Middlesbrough hometown. As we saw, it had been an area in which crime was rife and drug deals took place outside their back door. Today that crime is no longer an issue. In part, drug dealing had been tackled by boarding up the deserted building where deals were made, but the Shippeys felt that there was far more to it than that. Crime soars, they argued, when people are afraid to be out on the streets. But once an area is reclaimed by the public, drug dealers and criminals become easily identified and so they avoid those areas. Crime on the streets creates a vicious circle whereby the more people avoid public places, the more crime rises. It is only with creative acts of trust, such as practised by the Shippeys that a social fabric can change.

The neuroeconomics of trust

The prevailing assumption of many standard models of what are termed "rational economic agents" is that while individuals respond to incentives, when those incentives are absent then self-interest will prevail. For example, people will begin "shirking" work if they are not carefully monitored. However, in a series of studies conducted at the Center for Neuroeconomic Studies at Claremont Graduate University, Paul J. Zak and his co-workers point out most human beings do not function in this way and, for example, continue to work efficiently even when they are not monitored. A further example is that of investors who use a money manager, a situation in which it would be relatively easy to "cheat" an investor by the faulty reporting of the actual returns. A variety of studies show that while some rare and exceptional frauds certainly exist, and tend to get major news coverage, in the large majority of cases the exercise of trust is justified.

In countries such as Sweden and Norway two-thirds of people responded "Yes" when asked if "Generally speaking, would you say that most people could be trusted?" In a 2001 study Zak and Knack showed that a 15 percent increase in levels of trust within a country corresponds to a one percent annual increase in personal income. Applying those figures to the United States indicates that such an increase in trust would correspond to an additional $30,000 average lifetime income! On the other hand, if levels of trust drop below 30 percent then investment becomes so low that living standards stagnate or decline.[21] This provides a strong argument as to the cost-effectiveness of governments taking measures to increase levels of trust. These include such things as freedom of the press and civil liberties that promote trust in civil institutions. Even roads and telephones raise levels of trust by promoting social ties. When it comes to education, studies show that there is a 500 percent return on the cost of paying for an additional year of education.

In the context of laboratory experiments even randomly selected partners are found to exhibit levels of trust. In "the trust game" devised by Berg, Dickhaut and McCabe, students were paid $10 to participate in a laboratory experiment.[22] The rules of the game are first explained to a pair of participants. Participant A is then instructed, generally via a piece of software, to send part of his or her $10, (this could also include sending $0), to participant B. A is also told that B will receive three times the amount sent by A. Following the transaction B is then told how much A donated and is then instructed to transfer a sum, that could include as little as $0, to A.

According to the Nash equilibrium of the zero-sum game (the famous John Nash of the film, *A Beautiful Mind*) trust should not enter into the equation. One reason is that there is no sound motive for B to part with any of his money. Therefore A has no motive to transfer a portion of her own funds to B. This, however, is not the way the game works in practice for research shows that three-quarters of players A transfer money to B and an even higher percentage of Bs send money to As. In other words, when players exhibit trust they enter into a win-win situation where they both end up with more money than they started. In the original experiment an initial sum of $10 was used but in repeated experiments by other researchers sums as high as $1,000, and the equivalent of three months salary in developing countries, were involved.

Zak also conducted similar experiments, but in his case he also drew blood samples after A and B had made their decisions involving the transfer of money. The samples were then analyzed for levels of the hormone oxytocin which is associated with motivating pair bonding and care for offspring in small mammals. His research concluded that when levels of trust were operating between pairs of individuals, oxytocin levels doubled. He also noted that increased levels of oxytocin reduce the levels of stress hormones, so that when people are trusting each other they may also experience less stress. His conclusion is that an increase in oxytocin may produce a sense of temporary attachment and empathy to the other person.[23]

If Zak is correct in his hypothesis—that exercising trust involves a form of attachment between people—then this bodes ill for certain aspects of globalization. For centuries so many of our interactions were done at the face-to-face level and, as we have seen in the growth of science during the 18th century, for example, a person could visit a gentleman's home and observe his experiments at first hand. Likewise customers had a personal relationship with their bank manager. But today so much trading is done via the Internet in a totally anonymous way. Certainly people may continue to act in an honest and trustful manner but one subtle form of social interaction has been distanced—that more personalized contact that involves the mutual exchange of tokens of trust.

There is one additional point that can be made about Zak's experiments. His research program, which stretched over several years is, in essence, a challenge to the traditional assumption of "economic man"—a person who always acts in his or her own self-interest. Zak's results show that in case after case people will be generous, exercise trust and when funds are donated to them in the experiments they respond by transferring funds back to their donors. However he did discover a small number of individuals in the "B class" who did not respond in a generous way to the donations offered by the As. In one particular case an individual stated that he felt "elated" by the experiment while at the same time walking away with all the money donated to him and returning nothing to his partner A. In Zak's opinion he was the true "economic man". This returns us to the paradox of trust—that indeed it makes practical sense for us to run our lives under the assumption that we can trust those around us, but at the same time we may also encounter those occasional individuals who act out of total self-interest.

Cynicism

There is perhaps yet another factor that erodes the values of our lives and weakens our society. It is the sort of cynicism that often prides itself as 'being realistic" or "hardnosed". Let's face it, we are all a little suspicious of big corporations, so when one of them claims that it is trying to clean up its act, conserve energy, care for the environment, or attempting to take a more responsible social role, the general reaction can be, "We're not fooled by that, it's only window dressing". Yet I personally know senior people in corporations whom I genuinely believe to be ethically motivated, and to be deeply concerned about the environment, the well-being of their workers, the society in which they live, and the impact of their products on the general public. Yet at the same time there may be a destructive attitude of cynicism on the part of middle and lower management in the same company. The question I think we should ask is, just how "realistic" are the realists and cynics?

Set such cynicism against the remark made to me by one of the leading environmentalists in the UK: "What we once took as our enemies are now doing far more for the environment than politicians or even environmental groups."[24] Insurance companies, for example, know that climate change will result in increasingly erratic and unusual weather conditions, as well as a rise in sea levels and the flooding of seaboard cities. (Widespread and very serious flooding in England during the summer of 2007, for example, has resulted in a 10 percent increase in insurance premiums.) The very survival of these companies depends upon their pressuring governments and other organizations to do something about climate change. Certainly they are motivated by the self-interest of survival, but that self-interest forces them to take an active and positive response to environmental issues. Likewise if they want to stay in business, oil companies have to become energy companies.

Certainly there may be corporations in which corruption is found right at the top. There may be corporations whose sole interest lies in profit at all costs. There may be chains of stores whose goal in life is to eat up all the competition and leave a single vast monolith in every town. Yet it is my belief that many corporations do know the facts of life. Corporations know that just as with any animal, be it an elephant or a worm, they are part of a wider ecological system and, if they are to prosper, that overall ecology must also be healthy. This means that a vast web of life, the nested feedback loops, the plants and animals that depend on each other's existence, the retailers, wholesalers, suppliers and manufacturers must be fostered. In other words it is the "hard-nosed cynics" who are in essence being unrealistic and the visionaries who truly have their fingers on the pulse of events around them.

A corporation may take, but it must also give back. A corporation cannot ignore the writing on the wall; those are the rules of both nature and the marketplace, and no amount of wishful thinking can magic them away. An economy and a marketplace are very similar to an ecosystem, and just as the survival of a species of plant or animal depends on the health of that ecosystem, so too in the end the survival of a corporation depends upon the good order of the market, society and the planet itself. The terrible Irish Potato Famine occurred because British landowners relied almost exclusively on only one crop of food, which was wiped out by blight. Healthy ecologies survive on diversity and even an element of redundancy, so that when one species, or line of supply, is compromised, others are able to take over. Therefore even a degree of competition must be acknowledged in order to maintain a healthy marketplace. This is why corporations, if they are to survive, must face reality. And that means they must be willing to take a longer-term view of the world than politicians who think only in terms of the next election. That is why, in addition to profits, they must also give attention to trust, honesty and ethical action.

Social capital

Let us look at yet another context in which notions of ethics, trust and honesty can be viewed—the notion of "social capital". Robert D. Putnam is Professor of Public Policy at Harvard. Back in the early 90s he asked, in a famous study *Making Democracy Work: Civic tradition in modern Italy*,[25] why it is that the north of Italy is rich, with high employment and a wide variety of businesses, when the south is quite poor. Historically it was not always the case. The general assumption was that the north was richer because it had a more extensive infrastructure. However, Putnam's research indicated that its real source of wealth lay in high levels of trust, and what became known as "social capital". In short, in a region where trust is strong, people are willing to invest and take business risks. But the south of Italy was perceived as being low in trust, and so there was no healthy environment in which business could flourish.

Social capital is also about the ways individuals feel they can make a contribution to the society around them. Where social capital flourishes, people turn out to public meetings, they volunteer to help, form clubs and associations, and vote at elections. They feel that true democracy is possible and that a person can make his or her voice heard and affect positive change. Again this means that those people trust "the system". As usual these things are self-reinforcing, the more people trust the system, the more they contribute and the more the system generates trust.

At a recent conference on ethics in business, co-organized by the Pari Center, some criticisms were made about the way certain organizations operate and the need to change them. The response to this from one business leader was not one of cynicism but pleasure that "the system must be working". For if groups and individuals can protest and help bring about change, then a healthy social system must be functioning—by the very fact that individuals will think it useful to come together, form groups and push for change. If the system did not work, then either those individuals would be suppressed, or they would simply be disheartened that any change would be possible.[26]

The term "social capital" could be applied to the changes in social consciousness that occurred in Britain during the 18th and 19th centuries. In many cases they were the result of individuals who happened to have a strong spiritual or religious sense; many of them were Quakers. Life and society had a personal coherence and unity for them, and they used their wealth to build for the common good. In their early experiments they were therefore using capitalist-produced resources for pre-capitalist social values. Abraham Darby's experiments in Coalbrookdale, on how to smelt iron by using coke, laid the foundation of the Industrial Revolution. But Darby was not content to make money alone. He had houses specially designed for his employees. He laid out pleasant pathways for their walk to work, and established a college for worker education. Similarly the Cadburys developed a social security program for workers in their chocolate factory, and housed them in comfortable houses with large gardens. Other individuals made significant contributions to the society of their time, such as Elizabeth Fry with prison reform, and John Barnardo in the case of homeless children. At the age of 17 Florence Nightingale believed that she had heard the voice of God telling her that she had a mission in life, but it was not until she volunteered to nurse in the Crimean War that she discovered that her life's work was to create nursing as a trained profession.

Closer to our own time have been the examples of Schweitzer, Gandhi and Martin Luther King, Jr. Rachel Carson was inspired by her sense of our unity with the natural world and her book *Silent Spring* sparked off the environmental movement. E. F. Schumacher's *Small is Beautiful* introduced his notion of "Buddhist economics", which produced significant changes in the public's attitude towards growth and sustainability. Here in Italy, the late Ernesto Illy, chairman of Illycaffè, a firm that produces some of the best coffee around, was willing to pay above the going rate for coffee beans, provided that the supplier paid their workers a higher wage and ensured they had an education. And Illy did this, because he wanted to have the very best coffee, and that means coffee that has been picked by workers who are happy and whose dignity has been respected.[27]

Loyalty

Trust, honesty and ethics also breed something else; loyalty. I have known a number of business people who feel it important to believe in the inherent value of what they are marketing, be it coffee or shirts. They believe in their products and, in turn, rely upon the loyalty of their customers to expect the very best quality. A chain of retail stores in which these values operate, sets up strong and long-term links with their suppliers, and becomes known for selling only the highest products. In turn, the customer remains loyal to the store and to the brand. For all involved it is a win-win situation.

The business people I have spoken to still believe that the factor of loyalty remains significant; in other words, the trust placed in the product and in the store. However, today it is only one of a number of factors that would persuade a customer to enter a store, select a brand name, or deal with a particular bank. Where once a customer had a feeling of personal relationship to a store, or the "look" of a favorite brand, today things have become more impersonal and loyalty may be sacrificed in favour of price, or an image fostered by an advertising campaign. And, as corporations become increasingly global, what is the meaning of customer loyalty when a head office could be thousands of miles away in a different part of the globe? And how are customers and employees to have any sense of the ethical and moral stance of their board of directors?

How strong is the attraction of a bargain to an individual today, when measured against such factors as community responsibility, child labour, Third World sweatshops and companies with a poor reputation of environmental respect? So while loyalty still applies, it does not appear to have the same force that it once enjoyed.

This weakening of loyalty is also related to the lowering of standards of honest practice on the part of the public. It is not uncommon for a person to enter a specialist retail store in order to enquire about a DVD player, for example. They take up the salesperson's time, and have the benefit of that person's experience, yet with the full intention of later making their purchase from the Internet or at a cut-price warehouse. This slight erosion of loyalty and honesty that affects people's behavior in small decisions and actions, is comparable to a little cheating on the income tax return—the excuse of "because everyone does it" has a debasing effect upon the general fabric of society and undermines us all. It is the very reverse of Gentle Action.

This may be related to what the economic historian, Karl Polanyi, sees as our current level of motivation in life. In the past, most individuals were motivated by social standing, in other words by what other people thought of them and their actions. But more recently our sense of self worth, in Polyani's opinion, has been narrowed down to material wealth. Again, all this is part of the same vicious circle. We place our faith in wealth because we feel that our traditional belief systems are inadequate and even impotent to address the contemporary problems that surround us, just as we experience a lack of faith in politics or the importance of shared social values.[28]

Trust is good for you

Now let us join the realists and see how incorporating trust into the structure of a business will actually make it more profitable and socially acceptable. Take the case of a large UK retail chain, Marks and Spencer, with a market value of $34 billion. Its two founders were ethically motivated and, from its inception, it was to operate on a system of trust, loyalty and ethics. There was to be trust between the company and its suppliers, trust between employers and staff, honesty in the way the company operated and loyalty built up between the stores and their customers.[29]

The result was that the corporation operated with very low business costs. The more trust operated, the more profits the company made. By fostering trust in their relationship to suppliers, staff and customers the company experienced the following:

- In relationship to suppliers, there was no need for contracts, and much business was carried out via "gentlemen's agreements". In turn the relationship with suppliers was long-term.

- With staff relationships based on trust, there was no need to double check inventory on the movement of stock.

- There was no need to double check deposits at the bank.

- Theft by staff was virtually nonexistent.

- There was no need to advertise for staff, since people wanted to work for an organization they could trust and which had a good reputation.

- It was rare for the company to "let go" an employee. The vast majority stayed with the company for life.

- Staff spontaneously adopted responsibility and cost-cutting measures, such as turning off lights when they left stockrooms and washrooms.

- Whereas most companies spend 3-4 percent on advertising, this retail chain took out no advertising as it relied on its strong reputation and the loyalty of its customers.

- A shirt, for example, could be sold at £2 more than their competitors' prices because loyal customers trusted that it would be better made and harder wearing. Also, customers knew that no goods were sold that had been made by underpaid workers working in Third World sweatshops.

Trust made people feel good and was healthy for business, suppliers knew that they were dealing with a stable market, employers were happy, customers were satisfied, and the board knew that it was doing the right thing, and at the same time returning a healthy profit. This particular analysis refers to the period when Andrew Stone acted as Joint Managing Director from 1994 to 1999.

This experience is echoed by that of George Zimmer, founder and CEO of Men's Warehouse, a $100 million corporation with 600 stores around the United States. For Zimmer trust is the very essence of a good corporation, for when members of that organization genuinely have trust then they begin to share with each other. They share their knowledge, skills and experience and in this way a great wealth of generosity is generated within a company. As Zimmer puts it "It all begins to spiral upwards. Trust and honesty are the key".[30]

Restructuring corporations

In this book we have seen how organizations and policy groups can become more sensitive and creative in ways that would lead to the application of Gentle Action. In the case of businesses, however, an additional practical suggestion could be made. It comes from Andrew Stone, who was once the joint managing director of that retail chain of our previous example. Again it involves ways in which we can increase levels of trust and ethics in the marketplace.

Traditionally boards are composed of executive and nonexecutive members. The former are responsible for relations with suppliers, customers and staff; the latter are responsible to their shareholders. Lord Stone's proposal is that a third level should be added, one involving persons who would be directly responsible for the company's relationship to the community and environment. While members of a traditional board may happen to be ethically minded, the first responsibility of the nonexecutive board members is to their shareholders and the need to show profits, on the other hand executive board members must first and foremost think about suppliers, fostering relationships with employees and maintaining good customer relationships. In this sense concern about the environment, or a corporation's impact on the local community, would always be secondary. But, by adding a third level to a company's board, it now becomes possible to take community and environment more seriously. What is more, with a truly creative approach this third arm can actually make the corporation more efficient, more profitable and certainly improve its image with the public.

Of course traditional corporations take a cynical look at all this. "Yes, we need to appear to be socially responsible since that is good for our public image, but in the long run it is just an additional business expense we must shoulder." And so they form their committees and put someone in charge who is maybe not the brightest brain in the corporation, or a person they feel does not properly fit in or who is not particularly popular within the organization. However, Stone's argument is that this position should be filled by the very best and most creative people who will come up with innovative ideas that end up saving money and increasing company profits.

Let us look at the case of the fast food chain, McDonald's. Recently Stone came on board as an advisor in the UK and one of the first things he noticed is that they use a great deal of cooking oil. With a rapid turnover of food, the oil quickly becomes dirty and has to be disposed of. But used cooking oil can't simply be poured down the drain, or placed in plastic garbage bags, so the company must pay for its disposal, which adds to business costs and also stresses the environment. A far more creative solution is to have a waste product turned into a marketable by-product—in this case discovering a way that the waste can become the raw material in the manufacture of plastic. In one stroke a business cost is transformed into an opportunity for additional profits, and at the same time the environment benefits. What is more, new knowledge has been added to the marketplace that can be used by other fast food companies.

This is only one example, but think of all those corporations that make an impact on the environment, or whose operations impinge on a local community, or the society at large. What if highly creative individuals in those companies were not preoccupied with making returns for their shareholders, or marketing products, but with devising new ways in which they could interact with the environment, or make life better for their fellow citizens? It is the conviction of several of the business leaders I have spoken to, that taking into account the wider picture does not mean cutting back or reducing profits, it can mean the opening up of new opportunities and in the end lead to win-win situations.

On another note McDonald's employs a large number of young people to cook its hamburgers, french fries and chicken nuggets. How can life be made better for them? Well, young people like to travel so why not introduce a "McPassport". With this document a trained McDonald's employee can walk into a McDonald's in any European country and get a few days extra work to pay for their travel or hostel. This makes travel much easier for youngsters and provides McDonald's with a large floating population of trained workers. Again it is a win-win strategy.

Young people are also encouraged to continue with their education by taking an on-line test to grade their skills in English and mathematics. Employees are then given an on-line tutor and can even come into the store and take a mock GCSE examination. (GCSE is part of the British school examination system taken at the age of sixteen. These qualifications are useful when applying for further employment, or can be used to qualify for two additional years of more specialized education at A-[advanced] level.) If the student feels ready after the mock exam they can then go on to take the formal examination and obtain a valuable qualification.

And what about missed shifts and calling in sick? Well, if several family members have been trained at McDonald's then why not a formalized "family shift" system whereby the shift is not assigned to a particular individual but to any member of the family who can then come in and fill that time slot. Again a creative rethinking of the way things work produces a win-win situation.[31]

Globalization and the Internet

And now a word on that other bugbear of our modern world—globalization. In the time of Adam Smith and David Ricardo people believed in the presence of "the invisible hand" that would automatically regulate the market and ensure good economic order. Later Keynes demonstrated that there were certain things that an unregulated market could not achieve, such as full employment. Keynes's approach was based on ethical principles: that unemployment was a bad thing, that economists should cost in benefits and the public good, and that a world bank should help to assuage poverty in developing countries. It was a time when the British Welfare State was established to ensure that people would be cared for "from the cradle to the grave". Sound economic principles would ensure that a combination of a World Bank and the

International Monetary Fund would help to damp out undesirable effects in the market.

But, thanks to electronic communications, the modern marketplace has become vastly more complicated. International Corporations trade across national boundaries. Some are wealthier than many small nations. Stock markets are connected electronically so that trading is always beginning and ending somewhere within the 24 time zones. On the positive side, the Internet allows businesses to transcend national boundaries with total ease and the global electronic payments network accrues benefits to economies and people around the world. In addition, the widespread adoption of electronic payments has significantly expanded the sales volume of goods and services, reduced the barriers to immediate credit and liquidity, and eased geographic restrictions to trade and exchange.

In the 1950s the amount of money traded was three times more than the value of goods. Today it is thousands of times more and there is an uncontrolled flow of "hot money" across the globe at electronic speed. This means that our modern global economy has all the characteristics of a nonlinear system. And this is where the problem lies, for a nonlinear economic system includes such things as oscillations, periods of stability, and bifurcation points where a small perturbation can produce unexpected and qualitative new behavior. Clearly on a global scale this is undesirable. Indeed, we must face the fact that the global market may be inherently unstable. Already the effects of its oscillations are having a magnifying effect on economies as small fluctuations in the developed world result in much larger fluctuations in those less developed. Yet at the same time governments accept the inevitability of globalization, and in some cases appear to be renouncing some of their autonomy in the service of a worldwide economic system.

Such a state of affairs cannot be allowed to persist indefinitely. Uncontrolled speculation and the vast global flow of digital information must in some ways be addressed. There have already been some proposals along this line—the Tobin tax on the flow of "hot money", i.e, Internet trading, and the bit tax on the flow on data. But these have yet to be adopted by governments and agreed upon internationally.

With regard to the wider implications of globalization in all sectors of life it is clear that global agreements need to be established that are on internationally agreed principles such as presently exist in the field of, for example, whaling. There is a clear principle that life should survive on this planet, which implies the care of the world's oceans and forests, control of greenhouse gases and so on. Another moral principle would be that of condemning the exploitation of child labour. Yet principles that may appear universal from within the context of the industrialized nations, tend to be blurred in countries so poor that families selling their children into prostitution and sweatshops may be the one practical way for them to survive. Clearly the First World has a strong moral commitment to the Third, which may require agreements to be made at the international level.

In this debate one should not forget the other aspect of globalization, that of the notion of world citizenship, some form of world government, and international systems of justice. It would be a world in which people's rights and differences are respected. A world that is economically and environmentally sustainable, one in which true democracy is practised, one in which inequalities are addressed.

This moral commitment of the First to the Third World is not only to give help but also to learn how not to do economic harm. This applies in so many areas of economic life. Treaties may be decided by a group of First World nations without consideration of how these may affect the lives, work and economies of some developing nations. The American Revolution was fought on the basis of "no taxation without representation". Maybe a similar principle of "no treaties, no agreements, without representation" should be adopted. When trade agreements and treaties affect areas of the Third World; they should not be debated in the absence of those countries. There may well be corruption in some developing countries, but this so often flourishes through the active collaboration of individuals in the First World who offer bribes and favours in order to obtain contacts. Likewise we should ask who holds the majority of the stock in corporations that enlist child labour in their sweatshops.

Edy Korthals Altes, a former Dutch ambassador, told me of the case of fishing agreements that were being negotiated by the EU countries. On this occasion representatives from West African countries were present at the table but were in a position of particular weakness, in economic terms. In other words they were unable to protect the interests of other West African nations and the results were disastrous with thousands of fishermen being obliged to move to city slums or risking their lives by being forced to travel too far out to sea.

International agreements, regulations and controls are required to sustain a truly global market and economy. But ultimately these have to emerge out of a coherent ethical and moral system that is held by people of good will, people who are willing to trust each other and agree upon what they feel to be the common good, and the survival of all we hold important and sacred. Whether we are agnostic or deeply religious, this basis of thought and action must touch our deepest feelings of awe and respect for life, humanity, our planet and the cosmos. We may not believe in a particular God, but we do hold to something larger than ourselves, something that will persist after our death and should be preserved for future generations. In taking a significant decision the Iroquois people of North America do not consider the immediate effects on their children but what it would mean for the seventh generation to come after them. This would be an excellent maxim to apply in the face of accelerating globalization.

Trust and the Internet

In discussing possible instabilities in global markets the culprit appears to be the electronic age itself. But how new is the Internet? In some ways it is a version of older and trusted systems such as the postal service, the telegraph and telephone. But there is also a key difference. Those earlier transportation and communications networks were created under the watchful eyes of regulatory or legislative bodies, not only at the national level but also through international agreements. The Internet however was initially set up in an effort to create a US command and control system that would survive a nuclear attack by linking together computers in different parts of the country. In addition researchers and academics also created networks to share documentation. Those who worked on such systems in the mid-1960s could not have anticipated that a network would be created that would grow to one billion users and spawn such things as hackers, spam, sexual predators, and identity theft. Clearly the present system requires the implementation of a series of checks and controls. But it is a profound challenge to retrofit the Internet while at the same time allowing it to continue to expand rapidly. Moreover, since it is essentially global in nature it would require a series of safeguards and rules of conduct that are set at the international level.

Another issue is that of public and private space—we know that when we leave our home and go out into the town or city we enter into a social contract where we implicitly agree to be subject to certain rights and obligations. Similarly there are other spaces such as airports, shopping centres, sports stadiums, colleges, hospitals and banks where different sets of rules apply and an individual may, for example, be required to give identification. We have learned to negotiate the transition between such spaces and the different codes of behavior required. In a similar fashion the Internet offers a public space but in this case the rules of behavior are still to be developed. What is more it is so easy to move between public and private spaces in a cyber world that the transition is almost invisible. And this is where a major crisis of trust can enter for how much, today, do we trust the security of those spaces in a world of hackers and identity theft? And how much is e-commerce suffering from that lack of trust?

As Arthur Cordell and Prabir K. Neogi put it in their paper *Digital Economy: Issues and Challenges,* "Clearly it is of key importance to set in place safeguards that will guarantee a level of trust in e-commerce, banking and other commercial transactions...the cyber-infrastructure that is put in place has to be one that carries with it, at a minimum, the same degree of trust and confidence as the current infrastructure (physical, legal, institutional) developed for the industrial economy."[32]

Trust and self-organization

Earlier in this book, the marketplace was described as a self-organized system. Such organization becomes possible when matter, energy or money flows through a system. In the case of the marketplace, Jane Jacobs in *The Nature of Economies*[33] compares it to ecology. When the sun shines on a desert the sand heats up. At night this heat is radiated back into the dark sky and no self-organization takes place. But consider a forest. Here sunlight is trapped by the leaves using the process of photosynthesis. At night only a small percentage of heat radiates into the sky, the rest has been trapped by the system allowing it to become a sustainable self-organized system.

In a young forest dead leaves fall to the ground and become food for worms and insects, which, in turn till and aerate the soil. Rotting vegetation support fungi and other organisms. Gradually the complexity of the area begins to increase and shows ever greater diversity of plant, insect and animal life until it reaches a position of maturity where the self-organized system will continue to sustain itself—powered by the heat of the sun—indefinitely. In other words, the sun's energy is being circulated through a complex series of feedback loops.

Likewise in a healthy economy money, goods and services must circulate and so provide a multilayering of feedback loops that sustain the system. Clearly trust is the most important factor in maintaining the system. The more people exercise trust, the more complex becomes the web of feedback loops. But if trust were to be compromised then fewer and fewer people would be willing to deal with each other and the system would become impoverished, as was the case of southern Italy as analyzed by Putman.

Pari: barter and trust

Now I'd like to offer some personal reflections on the village in which I now live. Pari is a small, medieval hilltop village located some 30 km south of Siena in Italy. It has been around for a long time and once had been a settlement for the Etruscans. For centuries Pari had been virtually self-supporting. Food was grown locally. People kept pigs and sheep, and additional meat came from hunting. Clothes were made locally using wool, and cloth was made from the broom plant (fibre was extracted from the broom stalks after soaking them in the sulphur water of a nearby thermal spring). Wood was converted into charcoal for cooking, and building materials consisted of wood, stone, and bricks made from local clay. There were even iron and copper mines in easy walking distance of the village. People also knew of the power of medicinal plants and herbs that could be gathered locally.

With nature providing everything for life, the village operated on a barter system. In fact, until the mid-twentieth century there was very little money used in the village. What money there was, came from selling wine to Siena and smuggling salt past the nearby customs post.

In was only in the 1950s that the first cars appeared in Pari, which meant that people could now travel to Siena to purchase ready-made clothing and other consumer goods. Until that time people travelled by foot or on bullock carts which meant they had to spend the night in the city and return the following day. While today the *superstrada* goes straight to Siena, the previous road wound though many different villages. This change in lifestyle meant that people now became increasingly dependent on money to purchase goods. The transformation came about gradually and there are still stories in the village of the time when the local doctor was paid in food or wine. Yet while today everyone needs money to live, there is still a remnant of the old system that involves trust and obligations. We met this when we first rented a house in Pari and attempted to pay our landlady at the end of the month. She invited us into her home, offered us a glass of *vin santo* and a snack. As soon as we mentioned money she said, "Come back tomorrow". We met the same treatment at the local restaurant where we would be told, "Pay tomorrow...or next week". In fact sometimes it would be a month before we settled our bill.

I understood this as a way of cementing relationships, as a form of social exchange. Because you owe money to someone, this means that they are placing their trust in you and, in turn, you will trust them back. And so a great web of mutual trust sustains the village—feedback loops of trust if you will. Let me relate the case of a neighbor, Paolo. A few years ago we had to be in London for several months, during which time the insurance on my car lapsed. Paolo, who knew the insurance agent, renewed this for me. Later when I returned to Pari he introduced me to someone with the words, "This is David. He is a great friend of mine. He owed me 600 euros for two months."

This then is the life of a community that so impressed Claire and Gordon Shippey, a community enriched by a web of connections, a community in which people leave their keys in the door and greet each other by name.

Happiness

Certainly the values within Pari are far from those of Karl Polyani whom we met earlier in this chapter. His argument appeared quite convincing: We have become more materialistic, and so we have lost the older and more comfortable values associated with our grandparents, and think only in terms of prestige and money. It is probably something the cynic in us would like to believe when we read the newspapers and look at the people around us, for of course we, the author and readers of this book, would not share in those materialistic values! But maybe all this is far too simplistic. It reminds me of those figures governments produce (Gross National Product and Gross Domestic Product) to show that the economy is on the right track and we are all a little better off than we were a decade ago. Of course such figures have come under serious criticism by economists and sociologists because they don't take into account the degradation of the environment, the effects of crime on our lives, or the state of the nation's health. In fact they focus only on very limited aspects of our lives and do not take the whole picture into account.

So what about the values we place on our own well-being? Are they totally materialistic? Lord Layard is an economist who founded the Centre for Economic Performance at the prestigious London School of Economics. In 2005 he brought out a book, *Happiness: Lessons from a new science,*[34] in which he pointed out that we are much richer, in terms of cars, food, vacations, clothes, homes and income, than we were fifty years ago. Yet on the other hand we are no happier. All those material advantages do not appear to have improved our lot. Layard concludes that increased happiness should be the goal for a well-ordered society and suggests ways in which we could increase our general happiness.

In this Layard appears to be following in the steps of the Utilitarians, such as John Stuart Mill and Jeremy Bentham, who proposed that ethical decisions should be taken on the basis of "the greatest good (or greatest happiness) for the greatest number". This was, of course, a position that could be attacked on moral grounds in that the goal of producing a mild increase in the happiness of the vast majority of the population could result in misery for a very tiny minority. I would also suggest that happiness is only one of the goals that each of us would wish for. Another would be to achieve one's potential and be able to do what one really wants to do in life—that in itself may be a difficult path to achieve and would not necessarily result in extreme happiness along the way. Another would be to have pride in what we are doing, to realize that our work or relationships is of value to others. Then there are those who are involved in highly creative endeavours. From my experience of speaking to artists, writers, composers, actors and so on, when their work is really "flowing" they may not even have much self awareness of what they are doing, but are totally absorbed in the moment. In none of those cases I would say that one is "happy", but rather that one is totally involved with all one's being in something that is important and worthwhile.

But leaving that aside, let us turn to the British Government Well-being Working Group. A team of researchers and civil servants were asked to make a survey of research that had been carried out worldwide into the factors that are involved in having a personal "sense of well-being". The result was a 193-page report, released during the first days of 2007.[35] The motivation was to discover ways in which government policies could increase the general well-being of its citizens and, for example, look into the factors that cause some women to exhibit higher levels of depression. (The British Government has also launched a two-year research project into "Mental capital and well-being".)

While it is true that the criteria whereby "well-being" or for that matter "happiness" can be assessed may differ from expert to expert, nevertheless the results involve, as we would expect, a complex mixture of factors which fit well into the general approach of Gentle Action. There is, for example, no single factor—such as "reduce taxes", "give more money to sport", "arrange for longer vacations"—which can be imposed to increase our general well-being. The group found, for example, that those who took time to chat with their neighbors were generally happier people, as were those who stayed with the same partner and had regular sex. Other factors associated with well-being were: caring for endangered species, sleeping well, and not being overweight. On the other hand, a higher level of education, or having children, did not appear to increase a person's sense of well-being. Certainly a promotion or salary raise helped, but ironically it was even sweeter if done at the expense of one's fellow employees!

So well-being is a highly complex issue and again cannot be reduced to any single factor. It is not even clear that if staying with a loving partner and being sociable to neighbors increases our well-being, for it could be that those who are naturally happy and content are more likely to be sociable and form strong and lasting relationships. But all in all it does seem as if our general well-being stems not so much from prestige and material wealth but from a great web of intangibles in which we are embedded, a social ecosystem if you like. So just as a business, or a species thrives when the ecosystem is healthy so too our happiness and well-being may well relate to the community and society in which we live. It could be seen as an example of positive feedback: the better we feel, the more we relate to those around us and contribute to our community; the more we relate and contribute the better our community functions and supports us; the better our community functions the better we feel and the more we contribute. Again healthy communities and contented citizens are not so much the result of vast government plans or grants from funding agencies but from shared meaning and gentle action.

The story does not end there for in the spring of 2007, Cambridge University announced its preliminary findings on "happiness", based on the European Social Survey, which began in 2002. In this study some 20,000 people in different countries were asked to rate out of 10 their overall happiness and longer-term sense of fulfilment ("life satisfaction"). An additional survey enquired into such questions as their levels of trust, and degree to which people considered themselves religious. The Danes came out on top as the happiest people, with Italy, Greece and Portugal at the bottom.

The study concluded that overall happiness was related to the degree of trust that people had in the institutions around them. The Danes exhibited a high level of trust and also came high in the World Bank Governance Indicators. Italians however had low levels of trust in their government, police and legal system. Therefore trust is not only good for business but also for general happiness.[36]

But yet again it is not that easy to obtain "the whole story". Italians appear to exercise a low level of trust. Yet earlier in this chapter we learned that trust is very active in the village of Pari, where I have been living for the last twelve years. In fact trust is the cement that holds the community together and extends outside this village to an even wider network of trust. I have given the example of paying our monthly rent or the bill at the local restaurant. Then there was the time when we wanted to buy a washing machine and approached a man who works in Rome but visits the village from time to time. As promised he arrived with the washer, set it up in the storeroom under our house and demonstrated how it worked. We then asked him the cost and he told us simply to enjoy the machine and we could talk about payment next time he was in the village. A few weeks later he was back again and when we asked him the cost he simply wrote the figure in pencil on the top of the washer. I thanked him and said I would go upstairs and get the money. "Oh, don't pay me now," he said. "Give it to me the next time I'm in Pari". And so a mutual web of obligations is established between people who know and trust each other. Yet in Italy that web does not appear to be as strong when dealing with more impersonal institutions and organizations, a factor that appears to tie in with Paul Zak's findings that trust is strongest when based on interpersonal bonding. In turn societies and businesses are at their healthiest when this network spreads out to embrace an ever-widening community of trust.

✎ Reflections on Chapter 6

1. How does trust operate in your life? Try to go through your day and reflect on the many ways in which you "trust the system". That is, how many times do you assume that things around you, transportation, communications, shops, banks, medical services, schools, business transactions and even relationships will work as they are supposed to do?

2. What happens when you are outside your familiar territory? Are you naturally more suspicious about people and institutions or does your level of trust remain the same?

3. Surveys indicate that a person's sense of well-being relates to the levels of trust in the society that surrounds them. Do you feel this is true in your case?

4. Do you believe that if you trust people they will trust you back? Or will some of them take advantage of you?

5. How much trust do you have in the following:
Doctors
Lawyers
Politicians
Scientists
Accountants
Builders and renovators

The police
Emergency services
News channels
Real estate agents
Your bank
Your credit card company
Purchases via the Internet

5. What do you think of the old maxim "Keep your friends close and your enemies closer."?

6. What actions could you take to increase levels of trust in your workplace and the social organizations to which you belong?

7. Once when talking about Gentle Action a person in the audience, deeply concerned with the state of the world, said "But there is a fire out there. We can't wait. We have to do something now?" It made me think that, since the land around Pari is heavily wooded with some small outlying farmhouses, the first thing I would do is not run to put the fire out but see which way the wind was blowing, where it would be taking the fire, which roads would be free from smoke and so on. So suppose you saw a fire or other emergency in your neighbourhood. Think of the steps you would first have to check before you rushed into action.

Notes

Many of the discussions held with the Pari Center's network of business people found their way into this chapter including the May 2006 conference on *Ethical Choices in Economics, Society and the Environment*. For a report see www.paricenter.com/conferences/economics.php.

1. Umberto Eco and Carlo Martini, *Belief or Non-Belief?: A confrontation* (New York: Archade Publishing, 1997).

2. See, for example, http://www.telegraph.co.uk/money/main.jhtml?xml=/money/2008/01/24/bcnsocgen924.xmlf, accessed March 28, 2008. http://france24.com/en/20080313-banker-released-without-charge-france-banking-scandal-societe-generale, accessed March 28, 2008.

3. See, for example, www.the-shipman-inquiry.urg.uk and www.the-shipman-inquiry.urg.uk/reports.asp.

4. Article "Killer nurse addicted to thrills." see: http://news.bbc.co.uk/1/hi/england/oxfordshire/4919520.stm.

5. Information on the founding of the Royal Society came from discussions with the historian of science, Michael Bresalier. See also Steven Shapin, *A Social History of Truth:*

Civility and science in seventeenth-century England (Chicago: Chicago University Press, 1994).

6. For this report see: www.euractiv.com/en/science/eu-address-lack-public-trust-science-technology/article-135385.

7. www.royalsociety.ac.uk/downloaddoc.asp?id=3945.

8. "How to restore public trust in science", *News in Science,* March 16, 2000, www.abc.net.au/science/news.

9. www.ccepa.ca/news-trust_in_science_series.html.

10. F. David Peat, *Cold Fusion: The making of a scientific controversy* (Chicago: Contemporary Books, 1989).

11. F. David Peat, *Infinite Potential: The life and times of David Bohm* (Reading, MA: Addison/Wesley, 1997).

12. Reported in a number of newspapers, including *The Guardian,* see: www.politics.guardian.co.uk/publicservices/story/0,11032,954062,00.html.

13. For a report on this conference see: www.paricenter.com/conferences/academy/academy.php.

14. Article on the Metropolitan Police Act in the *Encyclopedia Britannica.*

15. Scarman Report, see: *Encylopedia Britannica,* also: www.news.bbc.co.uk/1/hi/programmes/bbc_parliament/3631579.stm.

16. Public Statement by Nuala O'Loan on her investigation into the circumstances surrounding the death of Raymond McCord, Jr. and related matters, (Operation Ballast), (January 22, 2007) http://cain.ulst.ac.uk/issues/police/ombudsman/poni220107.htm.

17. Onora O'Neill, *A Question of Trust* (Cambridge: Cambridge University Press, 2002).

18. Article on the history of the postal service in *Encyclopedia Britannica.*

19. http://complementarycurrency.org/ccDatabase/les_public.html, lists 167 examples of complementary currencies used worldwide.

20. George L. Kelling and Catherine Coles, *Fixing Broken Windows: Restoring order and reducing crime in our communities* (New York: The Free Press, Simon and Schuster, 1996).

21. "Trust and Growth" by Paul Zak and Stephen Knack, *The Economic Journal* April, 2001.

22. "Trust, reciprocity and social history" in *Games and Economic Behavior* 10, 122, 1995.

23. Paul J. Zak, "The Neuroeconomics of Trust", Social Science Research Network, August, 2005. http://ssrn.com/abstract=764944.

24. The environmental photographer Mark Edwards whose book *Hard Rain: Our headlong collision with nature* (London: Still Pictures Moving Words, 2006), on the condition of the planet has been sent to every head of state.

25. R. D. Putnam, Robert Leonardi, Raffaella Y. Nanetti, *Making Democracy Work: Civic tradition in modern Italy* (Princeton: Princeton University Press, 1994).

26. "Ethical choices in economics, society and the environment", May 5-6 2006. For a report see: www.paricenter.com/conferences/economics.php.

27. Conversations with Ernesto Illy.

28. Karl Polanyi, *The Great Transformation* (Boston: Beacon Press, 2001).

29. Conversations with Lord Stone of Blackheath, former Joint Managing Director of Marks and Spencer.

30. Conversation with George Zimmer at the Institute for Noetic Sciences.

31. Conversations with Lord Stone of Blackheath.

32. Arthur Cordell and Prabir K. Neogi, "Digital Economy: Issues and challenges" in *Journal of Internet Banking*, vol. 10, no. 2, 2005.

33. Jane Jacobs, *The Nature of Economies* (New York: Vintage, 2001).

34. Richard Layard, *Happiness: Lessons from a new science* (London: Allen Lane, 2005).

35. British Government Well-being Working Group, "Review of research on the influences on personal well-being and application to policy making" by Paul Dolan, Tessa Peasgood and Mathew White: http://defra.gov.uk/science/Project_Data/DocumentLibrary/SD12005/SD12005_4017_FRP.pdf.

36. See Cambridge University's website: http://www.admin.cam.ac.uk/news/dp/2007041701.

Chapter 7.
Gentle Action

In previous chapters I suggested that things start to go wrong when organizations or individuals take inappropriate actions however well meaning, and that this often arises because people do not really understand the complex and subtle nature of the various situations they face. In turn, an organization may be rigid and inflexible to the point where it is unable to create an internal image of the situations it encounters. One way this may change is when organizations or individuals allow themselves a period of "creative suspension" and begin to restructure themselves in more creative and dynamic ways that allow for the natural creativity and the tacit knowledge of their members to be fully employed. When this occurs then a new form of what I am calling "gentle action" may begin to operate.

I began to use the term, Gentle Action, several years ago to describe the creative sorts of activities and actions that could be taken when people are sensitive to the dynamics of their surrounding environment. It could be a form of minimal but highly intelligent activity that arises out of the very nature of the system under investigation.

As we have seen in this book, actions and reactions that proceed from conventional organizations, plans and policies can often be relatively mechanical in nature and are usually directed towards what is perceived as "the source of the problem". Moreover, the greater the change that is desired, the stronger would be the action that is imposed. By contrast, Gentle Action is subtle in nature so that a minimal intervention, intelligently made, can result in a major change or transformation. The reason is that such action makes use of the dynamics of the whole system in question. It could be compared to the way in which proponents of Japanese martial arts make use of their opponents' strength to defeat them. Rather than using violence, or dissipating energy, the martial arts expert directs small movements and uses leverage in order to focus the opponent's own momentum and energy in a new direction. In a similar fashion Gentle Action acts in a sensitive way to guide and refocus the energies and the dynamics of the system in question.

Another image of Gentle Action would be the minimal movements made by a person in the sea in order to remain afloat. Floating occurs, not through the expenditure of energy or violent movements, but by remaining aware and sensitive to the movement of the sea and the position of one's own body. Thus, by making tiny movements of the arms, legs and hands, the body can preserve its orientation. Surfing and skiing can also be thought of in this way.

Nothing new

Later in this chapter I will be giving some specific examples of Gentle Action in action but at this point I'd like to quote the old cliché that "there is nothing new under the sun". It is an important fact that ideas and truths about the world are continually being rediscovered and minted anew for each age. Thus if we go to ancient China we find the doctrine of *wu-wei* which is sometimes translated as "action without action" or "effortless doing".[1] In other words, the idea of reaching a state of equilibrium when we are in harmony with the Tao. Thus the Emperor will govern the country well simply by "being there", by sitting in his palace, with that palace having its proper geographical orientation with respect to the countryside, so that the microcosm becomes a mirror of the macrocosm.

Wu-wei is also compared to water which is weak and without any inherent form, yet has the capacity to wear away the hardest rock. Even when broken up into tiny droplets, water will reunite and finally find its way back to the sea. Likewise the enlightened person does not make an effort to exercise the will in order to resist the universe, rather he or she seeks to be in harmony with the natural flow of things. Instead of feeling ourselves as being separate from the universe, and seeking to exercise action on something external to us, we are connected to a universe that is in constant transformation. We live fully in each moment and seek to move harmoniously with that which surrounds us. Chuang Tzu compares this with wandering without a purpose. In other words, our actions arise out of the moment and are not motivated by any desire for reward, or to reach a predetermined goal. Thus many of the ideas and approaches discussed in this book find echoes and resonances in *wu-wei*.

Disappearing objects

Gentle Action and creative suspension are based on a general attitude towards rethinking the world, of not taking everything for granted, and being able to look in fresh ways. In this it reminds us of the physicist Neil's Bohr's notion that while the opposite of truth is a lie, the opposite of a great truth may be another great truth. So, for Bohr, reality was far too rich to be exhausted by a single, definitive explanation; rather we may require complementary descriptions that may even appear paradoxical when placed together.

It was Bohr who also played a major role in developing our understanding of the subatomic world. During the early decades of the twentieth century elementary particles were thought of as the building blocks of matter, somewhat like tiny pieces of Lego. But it was Bohr who argued with Einstein that we cannot really reduce the quantum world to "independent elements of reality". He even pointed out that the very languages we speak are a reflection of our large-scale world and contain assumptions about space, time and causality, so that "we are suspended in language so that we don't know what is up and what is down". It is language that puts a barrier on how much we can say about the "ultimate reality" of the quantum world. Likewise, physicists began to move away from elementary particles as tiny material objects into a world of processes, transformations and abstract symmetries. In other words, a radical rethinking of material reality was required.

Rethinking the ground rules was also something that happened amongst artists during the twentieth century. Traditionally, at least since the Renaissance, an artist had been a special sort of person who produced valuable objects. Admittedly there were also crafts people, such as metal workers and goldsmiths, who also produced precious objects, but the notion of "art"—frescoes, paintings and sculpture—was generally more highly valued; so art works were collected by kings and rich merchants and later found their way into the galleries of leading nations. To own a Leonardo or a Vermeer, was a mark of great prestige to an individual or a nation. But during the twentieth century a number of artists began to turn away from the notion of their work as necessarily being the act of producing precious objects.

One of the first to do this was Marcel Duchamp who came up with the notion of "ready-mades". These were mass-produced articles, which would be exhibited as "works of art". The most famous example was a urinal, bearing the signature "R. Mutt" and entitled *Fountain*. Others were a bicycle wheel mounted on a stool, and a bottle rack. Sure enough each of these became a "work of art" to be exhibited in a gallery along with more conventional "art works". As it turned out, the original *Fountain* was lost but careful reproductions were made and are today held in museums and private collections.

But if something purchased off the shelf can become a work of art, simply by passing through the artist's hand, then the whole notion of what is art is called into question. (I once saw an advertisement for mass reproductions of a Salvador Dali piece. It stated, "Each has been touched by the artist's hand". I imagined Dali sitting beside a conveyor belt with his arm outstretched!)

In the generation that followed, some artists became performance artists; others saw their own body as the arena of art. Yet other artists decided to work with the environment. Some sought to impose themselves on the landscape using earth movers and bulldozers. Others worked in more gentle ways, such as walking through the landscape or seeking to identify and care for the land. These included mapping underground streams, or species of trees, plants and animals within a major metropolis, repairing the dry stone walls of sheep folds, seeking to reintroduce ancient species of fruit trees and converting vacant city lots into wheat fields.

In each of these cases, artists have been questioning what they should be doing in the world, and what were the wider implications of their work. One artist who was particularly influential in this approach was Joseph Beuys who stressed the ethical and social obligations of the artist.[2] He introduced the concept of "social sculpture" in which he claimed that "Everyone is an artist". His "7000 trees project", for example, was a plan to plant that many trees in a German city, with the intention that this idea should spread to other cities throughout the world, as indeed it has. Thus ordinary people could become part of an art movement. It was also an invitation to everyone that they engage in the same sorts of questioning as the artist.

In this respect I am reminded of a story told by the environmentalist, Satish Kumar, about a woman who was given a very beautiful scarf. "But this is too beautiful to wear," she said, "I'll hang it on the wall." "That is the general attitude we face," Kumar said, "We hang beautiful objects on the walls of art galleries and live in dirty, ugly cities."[3]

Beuys believed that if our society were to be truly democratic, the present social system would have to be replaced by a "social organism as a work of art", something in which every person would be a creator, sculptor or architect of a new social fabric. Increasingly, and in so many other ways, responsibility is being placed on the shoulders of ordinary citizens who bear the task of co-creating this new "social organism", in the same way that during the Middle Ages architects, artists and crafts people would work together to produce a cathedral. Therefore the ideas of Gentle Action presented in this book go beyond the mere restructuring of an organization or aid agency, to the invitation to each one of us to take responsibility for the creative evolution of a new society.

Creative ripples

In chapter 3 we looked at the way a violent splash dissipates because each wavelet is moving at a different speed in the water. But when these wavelets interact and couple together they produce a soliton wave that will travel intact over long distances. As a metaphor for Gentle Action, we can ask what would happen if wavelets from all around the edge of the pond could couple together and move in a cooperative fashion towards some predetermined area. A major effect would arise not through an action that is external to the pond—such as the stone thrown into the pond—but rather out of the movement of the whole water. Likewise when a system, or a human group, acts as a whole in a coordinated way then a significant effect could be produced in a critical area.

While, in terms of ponds of water, this example is purely hypothetical it can certainly be simulated on a computer. What is more, it appears that the activity of the brain works in this cooperative way, with signals from all over the brain converging into one area and then spreading out again. To take one example, human vision involves processing units located in several different regions of the visual cortex, each of which is dealing with a different aspect of a scene—one looks at color, another for fields of movement, another at outlines, etc. Nevertheless, through what is called "the binding process", these various activities all integrate together to form a "scene" that we subjectively experience as "seeing".

When brain dysfunction occurs, these individual sub processes may not be fully integrated together so that some people gain direct access to these sub processes. In akinetopsia, for example, a person will not be able to detect movement as the rest of us do. They will "see" a road and cars, but without the experience of seeing the cars in movement. Water from a tap may appear frozen, so that at one moment the bathtub is starting to fill and at the next it is overflowing onto the floor.

As with that hypothetical ripple that arises from tiny fluctuations at the edge of the pond and moves inwards, so too in social or economic systems, action would emerge out of the natural dynamics of the whole system, arising in a highly intelligent and sensitive way and consisting of small corrective movements and minimal interventions. Rather than seeking to impose change externally and at a particular point in a system, Gentle Action would operate within the dynamics and meanings of the entire system.

Harmonizing

Russell's soliton wave of chapter 3 travelled for at least two miles along Edinburgh's Union Canal because, rather than its component wavelets behaving independently and moving off at different speeds, they bound together to form a collective. Something similar can happen in society when individuals are bound together through a shared meaning, so that a large number of tiny individual gestures harmonize together to form a great social movement.

In the same chapter we also learned of the "butterfly effect" produced when Rosa Parks refused to give up her seat on the bus. Its effect was to bring together 40,000 African-American citizens of Montgomery into a soliton wave that would boycott the bus system for over a year and initiate the Civil Rights movement. One or two individual actions would not have changed the system but when 40,000 people have a shared meaning it can move mountains.

Moving mountains is also what Peter Benson set out to do. In 1961 he was reading a newspaper on the London Underground where he learned that two students in Lisbon had been jailed by the Salazar dictatorship for toasting "liberty" in a café. Instead of rushing to the Portuguese embassy to protest, Benson went to St Martin-in-the-Fields church to meditate—creative suspension again. Then he discussed the issue with friends and spoke to the editor of *The Observer* newspaper, which later carried an article by Benson on "The Forgotten Prisoners", highlighting the fate of political prisoners of all persuasions in many parts of the world. In the article he proposed an "Appeal for Amnesty 1961". In this way Amnesty International was born, a movement that depended on private individuals taking a small action—just writing a letter—because they shared a common conviction, that people should not be shut away because of their political beliefs.

Where others would have mounted demonstrations, Benson's belief was that ordinary people writing letters to governments could make a major change. Julio de Pena Valdez, for example, was an imprisoned trade union leader in the Dominican Republic. He reported that after the first 200 letters arrived the guards gave him back his clothes. With the next 200 the director of the prison visited him. When the next pile arrived the director contacted his supervisor. When 3000 letters had come in, the President of the Republic was informed. And still the letters kept arriving to the point where the President called the prison and told them to release Valdez. Today Amnesty's membership is more than one million and has dealt with 47,000 prisoners of conscience.[4]

On August 14, 1980 an unemployed Polish electrician arrived late at the Gdansk shipyard where a strike had been planned. He was lucky to be late, for if he had arrived as planned he would have been arrested by the secret police who had been waiting for him. Instead Lech Walesa jumped over the wall into the shipyard and took control of the strike which was in danger of folding. The result was a sit-in that saw the birth of *Solidarnosc* (Solidarity) and a new life for Poland.[5] It was Walesa who acted as an inspiring catalyst to bind people together. And again, as we saw in the case of Rosa Parks, it was also necessary for the right context to be present for this social transformation to occur. In the case of Solidarity it had been the election of a Polish Pope that gave a new impetus to the people of that country to bind them together with pride.

Coherence

At this point I'd like to introduce another metaphor drawn from science and that is coherence. An electrical current passing though the fine wire of a light bulb causes it to glow with a white heat. Why does this occur? The reason is that the atoms in a metal are arranged in a regular lattice pattern, with some of their electrons being free to move through this lattice. An electrical current is nothing more than the regular flow of a large number of electrons, but as they move through the lattice they tend to bump into the atoms which produces two effects. One is to cause these atoms to vibrate, the other is to produce a resistance to the regular flow of the electrical current. The more the atoms vibrate the hotter the metal becomes and with sufficient current a wire will glow red hot or, in the case of a light bulb, white hot. And unless regular current is being constantly supplied from a plug in the wall, because of resistance the flow of electrical current will rapidly cease.

In a superconductor something very different occurs—the electrical current will continue to flow indefinitely. The reason for this is that at sufficiently low temperatures an extremely weak attraction between electrons causes them to begin to pair up and travel together. Soon the entire flux of electrons is moving in a totally coherent way as if, to use a colorful image, they had one mind. No longer do the moving electrons interfere with atoms in the lattice, they just flow past them leaving them undisturbed. In this way the resistance normally experienced by an electrical current simply vanishes and the current continues to flow indefinitely.

Something analogous occurs in superfluid helium. When water flows in a river it experiences resistance from the banks of the river which tend to slow down the flow. Likewise if there is a rock sticking up in the water, eddies will form behind it and the flow in that area will be turbulent. In each case the flowing water is experiencing a resistance and if it were not for the water that is constantly flowing down a hillside, or from a spring, and pushing the river along the water in the river would come to rest.

Not so with a superfluid. At low temperatures the extremely weak attraction between helium atoms results in the liquid moving as a whole. Where it encounters an obstruction it simply flows past in a smooth manner, without any eddies or turbulence. Again resistance to the flowing water has vanished and the superfluid will continue to flow indefinitely.

There is also another form of cooperation in metals at normal temperatures. The electrical repulsion between electrons extends over a very long range. But when each electron makes a small contribution to the collective (this is know as the plasma) it also finds itself relatively freed from the effects of this long-range force. In this way the collective is enfolded within the individual and the individual within the collective. Using electrons in a metal as a metaphor we could say that individual freedom arises by contributing to the overall well-being of the whole. Likewise the continued existence of the whole contributes to the well-being of each individual. What is involved here is not some large-scale program imposed from outside but the delicate cooperation of countless numbers of individual electrons.

In these examples an extremely weak attraction results in an astronomical number of helium atoms, or electrons, behaving as one and passing obstacles that normally hinder, without any effect at all. As we have seen in this book, nature supplies us with so many examples in which systems can behave as a whole—from soliton waves to superconductors, from self-organized systems to superfluids and plasmas. This should give us hope that real change is possible and that organizations, societies, nations and individuals need not continue to behave in fragmented ways, or take actions that do violence to societies and the planet. If we look to nature we find so many examples of order and wholeness that maybe it should suggest to us that Gentle Action is not some fancy, idealistic dream but a highly practical proposal.

In the sections that follow we will explore some more examples of Gentle Action before asking what each of us, as individuals, can do for the society in which we live.

Gandhi

Mohandas Karamchand Gandhi was both an important political leader in India and the father of nonviolent protest. Truthful or right action, for Gandhi, was governed by the principle of *ahimsa* which involved an openness to being hurt for one's beliefs, but never to do harm to others. In his book, *Gandhi's Truth*[6] the psychologist Erik Erikson argues that with *ahimsa* Gandhi was going beyond simply never doing harm, but also giving respect both to the other and to the truth within the person or institution that one opposes. We should therefore act in such a way that we ourselves are not only actualized, but also the ones we are opposing.

There was also an element of creative suspension in Gandhi's method. On learning of a particular situation Gandhi would tell his inner voice to "hold its breath" while he investigated the facts involved. These included not only the particular situation but its position within the much wider context of public and political opinion. To this end, Gandhi would visit the location and spend time living there.

Once he had a clear perception of the situation, and felt that it should be changed, he would make a wholehearted attempt at arbitration, for *Satyagraha,* or nonviolent action, should only be used as a last resort. If arbitration did not work, then Gandhi would prepare his followers who, before they acted, must be convinced of the rightness of their position; not simply on the basis of a clear examination of fact, but also that they were on the side of truth. Gandhi also saw a higher purpose than a mere resolution of some dispute. If a person who has been violating the lives and rights of others is filled with hate, then the purpose of truthful action will be to help that person to regain his or her capacity to love and trust. So *ahimsa* is not about attaining power or winning. It is in Erikson's words "the cure of an unbearable inner condition".

In chapter 3 we met the physicist Wolfgang Pauli who feared that modern science had become obsessed with "the will to power". Gandhi's method appears to be the obverse of this. Carl Jung pointed out that when eros is not present it leaves a vacuum and that vacuum will be filled by the desire for power. By contrast, Gandhi's approach involved giving respect to those who oppose us and seeking their return to wholeness.

In the West, Gandhi's nonviolent action is sometimes translated as "passive resistance" and here a word of caution must be added. There are some individuals who, in their daily relationships, exhibit passive aggression. At first sight they appear to be gentle people, never given to displays of anger. However, they have enormous skills in irritating the people they live or work with. The result is that they can generate anger and even violence in their victims and in doing so diminish and ultimately humiliate them.

Similarly when carried out in bad faith "passive resistance" can generate violent reaction in the people or organization it is directed against. Indeed, this is what happened in, for example, the march of Gandhi and his followers to protest the salt tax, a march where many were clubbed down by the police. Gandhi himself taught that *ahimsa* had not been invented by weak and defenceless people, but by those who could look their enemy in the eye. Nonviolent action was the method of the warrior who has conquered fear, and should never be practised by the coward.

Nonviolent action can take many forms—strike, boycott, civil disobedience and fasting. For Gandhi it should be the minimum action required to reach a given end. In the case of fasting, for example, Gandhi taught that it should never be used for material or selfish ends, nor to change the honestly held opinion of the person fasted against. Indeed Gandhi said that if fasting is done to blackmail a person into changing their position then it must be resisted against, even if it meant the death of the person fasting. Likewise the person on the fast should constantly be open to being shown that their position may be flawed.

In some ways Gandhi's approach evokes what I have learned about Native American justice systems. In the Western world courts seek to uncover legal truths and distinguish between the guilty and the non-guilty. In turn, the guilty must be punished and those not guilty exonerated. Things don't work that way in a Native American justice system. Suppose someone had stolen a horse or injured a family member. The result is that the harmony of the whole group has been disturbed. Native Elders will therefore bring the parties involved together and ask them if they can suggest some form of action which will restore harmony to the group. Once this has been discovered and agreed upon it is then presented to the whole group. The emphasis, therefore, is not on confrontation or punishment but on the good of the whole of which each member is a part.

Archbishop Desmond Tutu refers to something similar when he speaks of *ubuntu*, the essence of being human, which includes human harmony.[7] With the end of apartheid there was good reason for people to be angry and seek revenge and retribution, nevertheless South Africa came up with its Truth and Reconciliation Commission because, as Tutu, says, "anger and revenge" are subversive to the great good that is *ubuntu*. Indeed he relates the amazing story of a young white woman, Amy Biehl, who was killed by a crowd of young people whose motto was

"One settler, one bullet". The young men were arrested and sentenced to long terms in prison, however Amy's parents flew to Cape Town from California in order to tell the Commission, "We support these young people's application for amnesty". They ended up starting the Amy Biehl Foundation to rescue black youths who would become the victims of violence in the township. They even employed two of the men who murdered their daughter.

In the Native American context it is also worth noting that Western political philosophers Hobbes, Locke and Rousseau wrote of what they termed the "social contract". For Hobbes, early people who lived in "a state of nature" had no enforceable criteria for right and wrong, and their lives were "solitary, poor, nasty, brutish and short". Civilized society, by contrast, existed because individuals had come together and engaged in a contract between each other for their mutual protection and the good order of society at large. Hence, society was something that had been created out of the agreements of individuals, even if entering into the social contract meant a sacrifice of certain original freedoms. By contrast the Native Americans I have spoken to see the group as being primary and the individual as something that emerges out of the group.

Greenham Common

As we have seen earlier, in the case of Rosa Parks, Gandhi's approach had been embraced by Martin Luther King, Jr. It was also adopted by a group of women who decided to camp out on Greenham Common in the county of Berkshire some 45 miles west of London. Greenham Common was a piece of common land that had been taken over by the Royal Air Force during World War II for an airfield. In the years that followed there were many protests by the local residents about its use—first by the RAF and then the US Strategic Air Command. Finally, during the Cold War, and with the deployment of longer-range Soviet missiles, NATO decided to adopt cruise and Pershing missiles and 96 cruise missiles were sent to Greenham. The protests increased, particularly when stories began to circulate that, after a B-47 carrying a nuclear weapon had caught fire, radioactive contamination had been spread over the area.

Matters really came to a head when, in September 1981 a group called "Women for Life on Earth" marched from Cardiff in Wales to Greenham, a distance of 120 miles. There they delivered a letter to the base commander asking if they could engage in a debate with the camp on the issue of having nuclear missiles on the site. Their letter added: "We fear for the future of all our children and for the future of the living world which is the basis of all life."[8]

When the commander ignored their request they decided to camp just outside the perimeter fence. Living conditions were fairly primitive without electricity, telephone or running water; in addition they faced frequent evictions and vigilante attacks. Nevertheless they were soon joined by other women. Within six months they had gained considerable international press interest and became know as the Women's Peace Camp. The women practised nonviolent action, including disrupting convoys, to the point were some of them were arrested and sent to prison. Inevitably people became impressed by the authority of the group and several of the women challenged in the courts the legality of having the missiles at Greenham. Over the next 19 years up to 10,000 women became involved in the camp protesting the presence of nuclear missiles on British soil. In part, their argument was that the British public had not been consulted regarding their deployment.

The missiles left in 1991 but the women stayed on to ensure that the air base was closed and the land returned for public use. To this end the women successfully challenged the Ministry of Defence, as landlords of Greenham Common, in the High Court. Speaking on the BBC the Lord Chief Justice said "...it would be difficult to suggest a group whose cause and lifestyle were less likely to excite the sympathies and approval of five elderly judges. Yet it was five Law Lords who allowed the Appeal and held that the Minister had exceeded his powers in framing the bylaws so as to prevent access to common land".[9]

* For readers not familiar with British Common Law a *common*, or *common land*, is a piece of land on which people, often those living in the area, can exercise certain traditional rights that may go back for hundreds or even a thousand years. These would include, for example, right of access and the right to graze cattle. Other rights of a "commoner", were the right to fish, cut turf, or take wood needed for the home. Today the usage has changed somewhat and "the commons" are taken to be anything that is accessible for general public use, such as natural and cultural resources.

Knocking on doors

In the first chapter we met Gordon Shippey who went down the road in his neighbourhood knocking on doors, introducing himself by name, and in doing so transformed the area. Let us return to that example in more detail.[10] What I did not mention in chapter 1 was that his action took place within a certain context which allowed the "butterfly effect" to take wing. The area in which he lived had been subject to serious flooding. In 2000 there had been prolonged heavy rainfall to the point where Claire and Gordon heard what sounded like an explosion as manhole covers were blown out of the drains by the force of rapidly rising water. A few minutes later water was gushing through the Shippeys' front and back doors.

The local council was slow to take action—in terms of clean-up, testing for contamination of the drinking water, and prevention of further flooding. As a result, neighbors demanded that their elected council members listen to them. Gordon and Claire were amongst the first activists. But at these "flood meetings" the council dismissed their concerns as a freak happening, even when the residents produced evidence from an environmental agency that the houses had been built on a flood plain which had experienced problems for over forty years. Moreover, the issue was being exacerbated by inadequate drains, and the fact that the new houses being built in the area put even greater stress on the already over-burdened and outdated drainage system. Yet even with this evidence nothing happened. "Our problem was," said Gordon, "that at these meetings we were not a cohesive group, just a few individuals who were easy to ignore."

But once their community organization, TAMS, was formed those "few individuals" were united by a common purpose. As their organization started to obtain coverage in the local newspapers and on radio stations, the council was forced to admit that there was indeed a problem. They agreed that the flood system didn't work, and that concerns about health problems from contaminated water were genuine.

Working as a coherent group TAMS approached the council with an action plan that included asking for grants to fortify their homes against flooding They contacted inventors about flood defense—one had invented a type of plastic board that vacuum seals doors and windows, and another who had developed a fabric that sticks to air bricks.

Gordon writes "One evening recently over a bottle of red wine I was reading over what David Peat had written about Gentle Action. He used the metaphor of tiny ripples in water producing a big effect. It suddenly struck me that this was in fact a reality. It was water (the flooding) that had caused us to move into this area of community and Gentle Action. In retrospect the flood was both good and bad—good because when we came to Pari it gave direction to our thoughts at just the right time."

Gordon and Claire also felt that they were in a constant battle with the local council. So how, in terms of Gentle Action, did they deal with the provocation they experienced?

"We certainly feel frustration," says Gordon. "But as members of a group we have each other to talk to. Interdependence is the key. Also we decided from the beginning that whatever our feelings were at any given moment we must always keep in mind the wider picture. We must keep a steady support when dealing with issues—particularly when we are running up against the old order of things like the council. We are like water eroding away at a coastline over time, but it's not just an external erosion it's also internally, within ourselves. It means we are more flexible, more open to new ideas, we question things. We are not a token group like so many others. That's why the higher-ups do not like us. I believe that humour is also important—it breaks down barriers and leads to creative new ideas, like our flood defense measures, which started as a joke and ended up being a successful enterprise. By our actions we have changed not just the environment but also ourselves.

"TAMS is proud of the work it has done in raising the consciousness of the community about this forty-year old flood issue and support is increasing all the time yet the fight with the town hall does not abate."

One of their biggest achievements Gordon says is that, "TAMS is proud of being a mixed-faith community (Christian and Muslim) of all ages. We have found new friends and we talk in the alleys and streets. This sounds so simple but it has changed so much, anyone can call on anyone else in case of trouble or flooding. The great thing is that we have something which large parts of the world find difficult to bring about— this kind of mixed community. Our interracial group is working well and the council sees us as united—in other areas the pressure groups are either all-white or all-Asian. Perhaps what is needed to solve the world's racial problems is for local bonds to be made first rather than at the national or international level. Who knows? I wish I did. As for the future. Even if—and it's a big if—TAMS folds we still have our friendships and a community and that's more than any grant can give you."

Another example of how an individual can make a small but positive change is that of Jane Tinsley who had become exasperated with the way vandals were destroying an old stone bus shelter near her home in Fowey, Cornwall, England. The shelter was in a dilapidated state and the seat was broken. Jane's solution was to totally transform the shelter by painting the interior, adding a curtain to the window and even installing a rocking chair, wastebasket and pots of plants. Neighbors also donated paintings and additional furniture. As a result the vandalism ceased and the bus shelter became a popular attraction. One woman suggested that other people might like to "adopt a bus shelter".[11]

While I was writing this book Helen Goulden sent me another example of how an individual can make a difference. Helen has worked in a UK government department for several years but found that when she tried to start a conversation about the department's carbon footprint she was generally met with one of two reactions—that she was a "greenie" beating the same old drum, or alternatively the whole thing would become buried in the language of civil service red tape.

In the end she decided that what was needed was a "quite subtle and, importantly for me, anonymous, perhaps even wholly invisible action". And so she requested fifty water-saving devices from Thames Water Board and, by staying late after work over a number of days, she placed the devices in all of the toilets. As she writes to me, they are probably still there and saving a few hundred gallons of water per day.

Her next step was to think of the energy that was being wasted through unnecessary lighting in the toilet cubicles, since people didn't bother to switch off the light after leaving. She thought of putting up signs such as 'Please turn off the light' but this sounded too authoritarian. Was there a more subtle and gentle approach? And so, staying after hours again, she posted small signs under each of the light switches with quotations about light and lamps. For example Othello on contemplating the murder of Desdemona; "Put out the light and then put out the light". Another was "When it's dark enough you can see the stars".

The trick seemed to work and as long as the signs remained the lights were invariably switched off. Helen continues as a gentle urban guerilla, even slipping a water saving device into a restaurant toilet or a friend's bathroom.

Al Qurna

During the first half of the twentieth century Egypt imported concrete frame housing from Europe. However the architect Hassan Fathy pointed out that this was not only a costly process for the rural poor, but the structure of the houses themselves did not fit well into the daily life and cultural fabric of the Middle East. Indeed, he felt that modernity had brought about an unwelcome change in Arab societies, by moving them towards consumerism with its materialistic values, as well as a loss of contact with their traditions. He also felt that modernity had a particular appeal to the richer classes. Moreover it could be used as a tool to oppress the poor and dislocate them from their culture and history.

His solution, in terms of architecture, was to return to an ancient Nubian tradition and build houses, mosques and public buildings out of mud and straw. Despite objections that the houses would be washed away in the first spring rains, Fathy built the peasant village of Al Qurna near Luxor. Not only did he demonstrate the possibility of cheap housing for the poor, but also trained villagers in the techniques for building their own houses. He later expressed his ideas in the book *Architecture for the Poor: An experiment in rural Egypt*[12] which has led to similar experiments in other countries.

Yet Fathy's approach is not without its critics, who pointed out that the very people the village was designed for—in essence tomb robbers who sold artefacts to tourists—did not want to live there. Moreover Fathy's followers have ended up building elegant housing for the rich rather than providing housing for the poor.

One person can make a change

One of the most discouraging aspects people feel about the modern world is that they really don't count. In the face of multinational corporations and big governments a single individual can do little about changing the world. One voice will never be heard amongst millions. One appeal will never touch the hearts of those in the boardroom. And so a general apathy develops. A significant side effect of this is that in many countries fewer people are turning out to vote or to attend public meetings. Some look back to that mythic time of the "swinging sixties" with its dreams of new freedoms, student protest and social and educational experiments, but for most it is a period long buried in history, as remote as the dreams of the French and American Revolutions. As we have seen, sociologists and economists have developed the term "social capital", to refer to the benefits a society accrues when individuals take part in such activities, joining volunteer organizations, speaking at public meetings and voting on election day.

Yet one person can make a difference as this story, told by Edy Korthals Altes in his book *A Heart and Soul for Europe*,[13] illustrates. It revolved around a new approach to warfare in which strategists pointed out that it is far more effective to wound a soldier than to kill one, since a wounded soldier requires an infrastructure for support and therefore uses valuable time and manpower that diminishes an army's overall effectiveness. Far better, these strategists argued, a host of badly wounded soldiers than mass graves of dead ones. One approach to this end is to use laser weapons capable of blinding soldiers at a one-kilometer distance. Not only would a blinded soldier need help from his comrades, but the fear of being blinded when going into battle would be considerable. A number of articles and television documentaries appeared but did little to dissuade nations to abandon this approach until a 76-year-old Dutch woman wrote to Altes, "I have never belonged to any peace movement or taken part in any action but this cannot be done." She decided to act as a lone individual and ended up starting a petition that was sent to the Dutch Minister of Foreign Affairs. The end result of this one woman's reaction (together with a handful of other people) was that the Netherlands signed the 1995 "Protocol on Blinding Laser Weapons to the CCW Convention" designed to prohibit the use of laser weapons specifically designed to cause permanent blindness. One person can indeed make a change.

Heifer International: "Passing on the gift"

Dan West was a farmer in Indiana, USA, who, with others from his community, volunteered for relief work during the Spanish Civil war. They were given the task of distributing powdered milk to victims of the fighting. Often there was not sufficient for all who came and Dan and his friends had to make heartbreaking choices as to who would receive a ration and who would not. It struck them that it would make more sense to provide these people with cows rather than giving them cups of milk. This could make a real difference to their lives for rather than relying on handouts they would have a way of sustaining themselves in the longer term. His philosophy was based on the old proverb, "Give a man a fish; you have fed him for today. Teach a man to fish; you have fed him for a lifetime." He restated his own endeavour with the slogan "Not a cup, but a cow" and from this modest beginning grew a worldwide organization known as Heifer International.

West was a member of a religious group called the Church of the Brethren which had links to the Mennonites and Quakers and other churches opposed to war. The group helped to form the Civilian Public Service program, which placed pacifists in camps administered by Protestant peace churches. At the end of the war, in 1945, the Brethren decided to broaden their mandate with a worldwide program of aid to war victims and refugees; one in which hundreds of Brethren workers distributed millions of dollars worth of clothing, food, and medicines.

A year earlier, in 1944, West had returned to the United States and started "Heifers for Relief" by joining his neighbors in donating cows. This was to become a part of the Brethren's overall service program, and by the end of World War II thousands of heifers pregnant with their first calves were being shipped to Europe where they helped to alleviate hunger. In West's philosophy of "Passing on the Gift", each family that received an animal agreed to pass on its first female offspring to a neighbor who then did the same until all the farmers in a village had a cow to milk. Male calves were kept for meat that improved a family's diet or could be sold for income. This income was vital for the purchase of materials needed to rebuild what had been destroyed during the war.

Politics seemed to vanish where these animals were concerned. In *To Serve the Present Age: The Brethren Service Story*, Thurl Metzger writes, "Among the historic events of that period was a shipment of cattle to the Soviet Union in 1956." This shipment was accompanied by several representatives who were received by the Ministry of Agriculture and, as Metzger continues, "Though this was a period of political tension we were graciously received with genuine hospitality, giving credence to M. R. Zigler's (executive secretary of the Brethren Service Commission) frequent statement that '...you can go anywhere on the back of a heifer...'" In addition animals were sent to Hokkaido to be used by Japanese farmers released from Russian prisons following World War II.[14]

Today Heifer International is involved in distributing over 25 different types of animals, from silkworms to water buffaloes. They are particularly concerned to provide what they call "7-M Animals". These are animals such as goats, water buffalo and camels that provide meat, milk, muscle, manure, money, materials and motivation. The animals are purchased from local dealers who supply livestock that can thrive under local conditions. Members of the community choose the livestock they believe best for themselves. In addition, Heifer is involved in contributions of trees to restore woodlands and seeds for forage to build the foundations for an environmentally responsible stewardship of the land and water resources. Training is another gift that is passed on as more members of communities prepare to receive gifts from their neighbors.

To take a recent example, following the violence in Rwanda, Heifer International is helping families to reestablish themselves with gifts of cows and offering training in their care. While Dan West's original model is the same, in this context "Passing on the Gift" means that members of ethnic groups so recently at war must now rely on each other for the livestock and training they need to rebuild their lives. Heifer livestock is therefore not only a source of much-needed food but is creating bonds of cooperation between Hutus and Tutsis.

Heifer International has helped 38 million people in 125 countries to become self-sufficient. Yet it all began with a simple insight by someone working right in the field, rather than a committee or government program supported by a large budget and located in some office thousands of miles away.

There was yet another spin-off from the work of West and Zigler, for the Brethren also began to explore ways in which voluntary agencies could relate their personnel and expertise to government programs in developing areas of the world. As a result, International Voluntary Services was created in 1953 which became the prototype for the US Peace Corps formed in 1961.

Gaviotas

In the early 1970s a group of Columbian researchers, students, and labourers dissatisfied with the political turmoil and urban decay, decided to build a new town in what was considered uninhabitable pampas. Their idea was to create a totally sustainable community. One of the prime movers in creating Gaviotas was Paolo Lugari who said they wanted to do something "For the Third World by the Third World" and "When you import solutions from the First World, you also import their problems". The people involved wanted a chance to plan their own tropical civilization from the ground up, rather than importing models and technology from the northern countries.

Thanks to the cooperation of a number of universities, who sent out their students, many ingenious low-tech devices were created. For example, the energy generated by the children's see-saw was used to power water pumps. The community also planted many trees so that the surrounding barren land was gradually converted into a forest. Today Gaviotas is totally energy independent. The community farms organically and uses wind, solar power and a wood-powered turbine. Every family enjoys free housing, community meals, and schooling. There are no weapons, no police, and no jail. There is no mayor. The village is populated with peasants, scientists, artists and former street kids. The United Nations named the village a model of sustainable development.[15]

Grameen Bank

Muhammed Yunus is an economist who had studied at Vanderbilt University, on a Fulbright scholarship and sought to bring economic reforms in Bangladesh. In 1976 as he was walking through the village of Jobra he spoke to Sufiya Begun, a woman making bamboo stools in a market. She explained that she had to buy the materials from a middleman and then sell back the finished stools to him so that she ended up with a profit of two cents on each stool. He asked her why she didn't go to a money lender and borrow some money to buy her own raw materials but was told that money lenders charged 10 percent per week, and in one neighbourhood 10 percent a day.

On the following day he asked one of his students to make a list of people like Sufiya working in the village who were dependent on traders. The list came to 42 people who, for a mere total of $27, could buy their own materials and become independent of traders. Yunus handed his student the $27 and asked her to distribute it amongst the women. At that moment the notion of microcredit was born.[16]

On the following day, Yunus went to a branch of the Janta bank, a Bangladeshi government bank, to explore the possibility of the bank giving very small loans to poor people to help them work independently. The bank manager began to laugh at the impossibility of such an absurd idea. The amounts of the loans involved would not even cover the costs of filling out the loan documents and, what is more, most of the people would be illiterate and incapable of filling out the forms and signing their names.

In the end Yunus decided to create his own bank, the Grameen bank, that would involve itself in small loans, generally given to women, who could use the money to buy things that could be used to produce goods to sell at the market, such as sewing needles and thread to become tailors and seamstresses; chicks to raise for meat and eggs to sell.

The initial loans were very small amounts of under $100. As the women paid back the loans, this allowed more women to borrow and start their own businesses. Women were chosen, since in these cultures they were better credit risks than men and they spent the money they earned on better food, clothing and education for their children, rather than on imported goods. In fact the rate of repaying loans was higher in the case of poor women than with the more well-off. In this way money stayed within the village which began to prosper. The Grameen bank now belongs to 2.4 million borrowers, 95 percent of them women. It has dispensed a total of $5.5 billion in small loans averaging $235 each.[17] Today Yunus's scheme of microcredits has been adopted in many countries.

He was even invited by the US government to set up a microcredit system in Arkansas. In 2006 Yunus was awarded the Nobel Prize.

Microphilanthropy

The notion of microphilanthropy follows on nicely from the example of the Grameen bank, but this time it was only made possible through the existence of the Internet. The concept can be illustrated via the experiences of one of our visitors to the Pari Center, Christine Davis Egger. In May 2006 she happened to read an online news article about a boy in Nepal, Yubaraj Khadka, who had been working to support his family since the age of twelve. Seventy people posted comments to the article saying they'd help support his education provided that someone could find him and deliver 100 percent of that support to him directly, rather than though some nonprofit organization that would need to use part of the funding to cover its overheads. Christine was so struck by the story that she decided to "make this happen", both for the boy's sake and for the people who voiced a desire to help.

Over the next year, she worked with a small group of volunteers to find Yubaraj. They met with his family and arranged for tutoring, school exams, and financial support so the family could afford to allow Yubaraj to return to school. Christine and her friends then used the Internet, via http://hotzone.yahoo.com, to tell the people who had voiced a desire to help that it was now possible. Another website, http://yubaraj.givemeaning.com, allowed people to donate funds, and http://www.for-yubaraj.blogspot.com was used to communicate openly and regularly on everything the group was doing. Yubaraj was enrolled in school in April 2006 and he's been a full-time student ever since.

Microphilanthropy (also called P2P or peer-to-peer philanthropy) refers to small, direct interactions between people who are giving and receiving philanthropic support, especially where that exchange is facilitated by Internet technology. It is based on the definition of philanthropy as "the love of humanity" and embraces a wide range of activities including donating funds for very specific causes, volunteering, emergency response activities and even mentoring. It has also given rise to a number of new sites including GiveMeaning.com and ModestNeeds.org, as well as to fund-raising tools on social networking sites such as Facebook.com.

As Christine Egger puts it, "Individually and collectively, these direct gestures of caring have the potential to serve as a kind of Gentle Action if the field of meaning from which the desire to act is our shared humanity. If the field of meaning is more limited than that— emphasizing the national, cultural, or economic identity of the giver or receiver, for example—then the gesture becomes "action from the outside" with the potential to do harm. But so long as the giver and receiver both reside inside the action—so long as they're both held in equal measure as co-creators of the desire to act and the act itself—then the philanthropic action becomes gentle and positive for both the giver and receiver.

The Internet provides a tremendous opportunity to reach across boundaries and connect with one another as people first, and to engage in philanthropy as Gentle Action on a greater scale than ever before."[18]

Each one teach one

Paulo Freire worked with the illiterate poor in Brazil. In doing so he began to develop a personal philosophy that was similar to that of liberation theology, for he felt that this group had become marginalized into "the cultures of silence". It turned out that literacy was a requirement for voting in a Presidential election so when, in 1961, he became director of the Department of Cultural Extension of Recife University, he began an experiment in adult literacy. In 45 days, 300 sugar cane workers were taught to read and write. His considerable success arose because he realized that it really did not make much sense to teach literacy as a skill that a person "should have" in the absence of any particular context. Rather literacy became a doorway into political participation. People were highly motivated to read, for it was a way for them to gain political emancipation. As a result, thousands of cultural circles were created across Brazil. Then in 1964 a military coup took place and for a time Freire was imprisoned. From Brazil he moved to Chile where he continued his literacy work. As a result, UNESCO acknowledged that Chile was one of the five nations of the world which had best succeeded in overcoming illiteracy.[19]

Freire's work had also had a profound effect on educational theory in the United States and elsewhere. In his "Each one teach one" approach, an illiterate person, once taught the skills of reading, must then pass them on to others. In this way an ever-spreading movement of education is created. His philosophy of education was also to break down that distinction between teacher and student and reject the idea of a student as a sort of receptacle to be "filled with knowledge". Rather, the basic relationship would be teacher-student and student-teacher: For the teacher would also learn and the student teach. Clearly Freire's own theories, which form the basis of so many "grassroots" educational programs across the US and Canada, was the result of something taught to him by the rural poor and dispossessed.

One example of ways in which the teacher-student relationship can be transformed involved an academic living in a Canadian city who was paired, through a volunteer literacy program, with an Inuit man who wished to learn to read. The academic had previously learned that an igloo is not the cold, icy place we all imagine but in fact can be so warm inside that outer clothing can be shed. Thus he was not too surprised when he found the heating set on high in the man's apartment. He was, however, a little unnerved to discover that they should both take off their shirts and sit close together with their flesh touching. The lesson proceeded for around twenty minutes at which point the Inuit man said that it was time to sing some songs. On other occasions he would explain how to hunt, and the way whales were being frightened away by the sound of machinery and motorboats in his small village. He also promised his teacher that, should he ever visit, he would give him a meal of "raw seal guts", a great delicacy. Thus the Inuit man began to learn to read, while his teacher realized that there were different ways to structure the process of teaching and at the same learned a great deal about Inuit culture.

At this point I'd like to add a little qualification about a society achieving the ability to read and write. Again in this book we have seen that there are two sides to every action. Yes, we can feed the hungry, but at a price to them. Yes, we can provide better housing but at the same time disrupt a close-knit society. So what about the "power of illiteracy"?

Handsome Lake of the Seneca people had led a somewhat dissolute life until one day, in 1799, he fell into a deep coma during which the Great Spirit began to teach him. When he returned to consciousness he passed on the teachings and initiated the White Dog Feast. The teachings spread not only amongst the Seneca but to other members of the Iroquois confederation of nations. Right into the twentieth century the Code of Handsome Lake was passed on orally in the Long House and took four or five days to recount. Yet with the advance of literacy people no longer have the ability to memorize long stories and pass on oral history to the next generation.[20]

Along with literacy comes numeracy. In Afghanistan, women used to be able to simply look at a person and then make a perfectly fitting dress or suit for them. I remember attending a conference on literacy in Canada. One of the speakers had worked in Afghanistan in the early 70s before the Soviet invasion. "As well as literacy we taught them numeracy and how to use the metric system," she said proudly. "So now they are able to use a tape measure when making clothes." However, when questioned she admitted that their traditional skills had disappeared. In the Middle Ages people were taught "reckoning". That is, the ability to judge weights accurately by hand and volumes of irregular shaped objects by eye. I have also heard stories from people from India that their grandmothers used to be able to do this, and how the clever grandchildren would check out their grandmother's estimates with a set of scales or a measuring jug.[21]

Certainly no one would want to turn the clock back on literacy, but we should also recall that just as species are being wiped out at an alarming rate, so too are oral histories, local knowledge, and even entire languages are being lost.

Native American talking circle

Non-natives often wonder how decisions are made within an indigenous community. In a talking circle a pipe or feather may be passed around, allowing each person to speak in turn. The topics discussed are not so much plans or proposals but people's feelings, memories, ancient stories. At first sight this appears puzzling until one realizes that a field of meaning is being created which is owned by the whole group, rather than by the particular individuals who speak. In one sense their remarks are personal, in another they are an expression of the rich dynamics of the group.

In the end no formal decision is made and no detailed plan agreed upon, but somehow each person "knows what to do." Action arises out of the group as a whole, not through the instructions of an elected leader. (Although for certain tasks a leader may be appointed, this authority always exists as an expression of the group and will therefore vanish once the task has ended.)[22]

Changing hospital attitudes

Therese Schroeder-Sheker began life as a professional musician who worked with the medieval harp. She had also had the experience, while a student working in a nursing home, of attending a death and actually climbing onto the bed and holding the dying person, an event that became very important to her. Her musical research involved an investigation of the practices at the Abbey of Cluny in France during the 10th Century. There, as in other centres, the monks had a pharmacopoeia involving healing plants and herbs. But what was exceptional was the second pharmacopoeia that contained prescriptions of musical modes for use in illness. In particular, when a monk felt that he was about to die the other monks would gather and chant in his cell.

Therese decided that she would adopt this practice in a modern hospital setting to work with the dying. At first she worked in Colorado, then moved to St Patrick's hospital in Missoula, Montana, where she ran the Chalice of Repose Project. Only if invited would two harpists enter a patient's room and play and sing over the dying person. Therese spoke of weaving a tonal substance over the body, so that even if the person were in a coma the music would enter through the skin and do its work. At first minor modes were used and then at the moment of death, or "transitus" as Therese prefers to call it, the major modes would herald the release of the spirit. Therese's work invites a number of metaphors. One is of "sacred midwifery"; that is, the musicians are aiding in a transitus, which is a birth of the soul into a new life. Another is that of alchemy, since the music enters the body and acts to separate the subtle (the spirit) from the gross (the physical body).

Initially some of the doctors in the Missoula hospital were rather suspicious of what she was doing, for it all seemed to them rather "New Age". Yet Therese insisted that the deaths be medically monitored and a proper study made. Gradually the doctors came round to her way of thinking as they discovered that patients could be given an easeful death, even to the point of being removed from painkillers.

Therese also noticed that doctors were only very rarely present at a death. After all, for a physician, death represents a failure. Moreover it was hospital policy that the body should be removed and the bed made ready for the next patient within 30 minutes. But, as her work progressed, she noticed that doctors began to attend the deaths of their patients. What is more, relatives were allowed to stay with the body for an hour or so. In short, she radically changed the whole attitude to death in that hospital. In turn, her students have entered other hospitals across the state and her movement is expanding across the United States.[23]

Enterprise Facilitation

I began this book with an example from Ernesto Sirolli's experience of how much damage can be produced by the desire for "doing good". It was therefore a great pleasure that as I was working on the final version of this book that Ernesto should visit Pari and the Pari Center. While it was only a short visit, Ernesto impressed everyone with his passion and energy, as he explained his approach of Enterprise Facilitation, and related a number of stories of the ways in which we have interfered and damaged communities with our desire to help.

Sirolli's Enterprise Facilitation is based on the fundamental premise that we should do nothing until we are specifically asked for help by a community. Even if we see that things are going badly wrong, even if we are convinced that we know the best way to help a village or town, we should not act until we are invited to do so. To enter a community, and impose a well-meaning solution to what we perceive as a serious problem is, in Ernesto's words, either total arrogance or neocolonialism. And these, he felt, are the traits that characterize so much of what we do in the West. We have not learned to simply wait and listen, and suspend our desire to help until we are specifically asked.

As he explained how he and his colleagues work he related with a host of examples where factories or technologies had been donated to developing nations by the West to the eventual detriment of a country's infrastructure. In many cases the technology donated is obsolete by standards of the West. This means that the manufactured goods produced may be judged as inferior in the Western market and so that country will have difficulties in exporting and selling its products. Aid of this kind can also create dependencies. A Canadian aid agency exported a bread-making facility. This was accompanied by the donation of Canadian wheat. The result was that, unable to compete, the local bakeries closed down with resulting unemployment, and the country had become dependent on Canadian wheat.

In another example a young Canadian was sent north of the Arctic Circle to work with a local Inuit community. When he arrived he noticed that a great deal of heat was escaping from the unit that supplied heat to the community. This gave him the idea that something useful could be done with that wasted energy, and he spent several months researching possibilities. Finally he felt he had the ideal solution and called a meeting of the community leaders. At this meeting the young man unveiled his plans and displayed a series of drawings. He told them how he could arrange to have a large greenhouse assembled around the heat unit. Inside this greenhouse it would be possible to grow a variety of vegetables, and so the local community would be provided with fresh vegetables all year round.

When he had finished he was faced with a group of impassive faces. He waited until one of the men said, "Who are we?" "Well, you are the chiefs," he replied. The man nodded, "Yes, but who *are* we?" "Well, you are Inuit," the young man said. Then came the reply "And do Inuit eat vegetables?" Of course vegetables are simply not part of their diet. So again another plan, luckily this time not actually realized, was based on both good intentions and ignorance.

Sirolli's own approach is that, when asked for help by a community, he will send in a trained facilitator and ask several members of the community to introduce the facilitator to their friends and relatives. The facilitator has no office, and explains that if someone needs help he will be happy to come to their home and talk with them. The facilitator then simply sits and waits for weeks, or months until someone asks for help. The facilitator hopes to meet someone who has a wonderful idea for a new project, a plan to make a new product, or to offer a service that the community really needs. He is waiting to meet a person with vision and energy. His role at this point is to offer assistance, but only when invited. For example, the individual may have a fantastic product but no idea how to market that product. It is the role of the facilitator to bring that person in contact with someone in the community with a flair for marketing. Or it may be that a person has a great service to offer but no head for finance, and therefore needs to team up with a good financial advisor. Above all, the facilitator is not a "business consultant". He or she is not there to tell anyone how to run their business, or what they should be doing, but simply to listen and bring the right people together at the right time. When this is done the enterprise will take off on its own steam.

In this sense Sirolli's approach is very much in line with the Gentle Action proposed in this book. The new enterprises and services that arise and flourish in a community are not the result of some central government policy, foreign aid, or individuals who tailor a grant proposal to fit in with a foundation's mission statement, but rather are born out of the community itself, the needs it knows best, the web of interconnections amongst its members, and the natural creativity and passion of one or two individuals who have come up with a brilliant new approach that needs realizing.

What can we do?

We have seen a number of examples of Gentle Action in action, ways in which a particular individual, working within a given situation, has discovered new and creative measures that can spread within a system or society. So what can each one of us do in our own lives, families, work and community to help bring about Gentle Action and creative change?

I suppose at this point in the book we should expect to see the "Seven Steps to Gentle Action" but if I, as author, took this route I'd simply be doing the very thing that I have criticized from the start— standing outside a system and making up a series of rules and suggestions for action. So why not let other people have a chance to talk and see what they propose?

In the spring of 2007 I was in Canada speaking in the province of Alberta. Alberta is a particularly rich province because of its oil and people there were concerned about its future as well as the responsibility they had for their natural resources. I found people to have a very positive approach to their future yet on the other hand there was also a degree of distress expressed by people who worked for governments and large organizations. On a daily basis they face enormous problems and vast issues. As a result they felt it was simply not practically possible to encompass the full extent of a particular issue and, as a result, issues were divided up to the point where a person could approach one part of a problem as "do-able".

At first sight this is a workable approach yet at the same time certain aspects of a particular situation are deeply interconnected to others with feedback loops taking the results of an action in one area and amplifying its effects in another. So clearly just focusing on "do-able" parts of a problem is going to result in fragmentation.

Maybe the solution is to imitate the human vision system with its dual functions of high-level discrimination at the yellow spot, along with a peripheral vision that is sensitive to movement. Or Whitehead's notion that the mind employs both context-dependent perception, which is sensitive to meaning and interconnection, along with a perception that is highly focused on detail yet less aware of overall meanings.

In other words we must replace fixed strategies by process approaches involving movement—a constant dance forward into the "do-able" parts of a problem and then back to take into account the overall context and meaning of the much wider issue. It is a dance that must be performed both by each individual and the organization as a whole.

During my visit I was invited to give an evening talk to an audience in Calgary that included teachers, community leaders and those generally concerned about the future. On the following day these people divided into a series of groups to discuss together and come up with some ideas and recommendations. What follows is a summary of some of the things they said, some ways in which they felt they could contribute towards a Gentle Action.

- Maybe rather than always seeking to come up with answers we should be looking for good questions.

- We all need to take much more personal responsibility for what is going on around us. We need to make Gentle Action something personal.

- We need to exercise gentler connections rather than looking for quick fixes.

- We need more trust in society. In so many ways we already place great trust in things we don't particularly bother about such as driving on the highway and simply trusting that the oncoming driver won't swerve and hit us.

- We must care for the earth and the region in which we live. We must realize that we belong to the land and the land does not belong to us.

- We need to create organizations that will honour our spirit and will allow us to express our individuality.

- We must learn to honour wisdom and in particular the experiences and advice of the oldest members of our society.

- We must give more attention to the ethical and moral dimensions of the decisions we make and the actions we take.

- We must ensure that all members of our society are empowered.

- We must never forget the importance of family and community connections.

- Each one of us can do something very significant with a tiny action.

- We must never forget that the butterfly effect involves not only one small but significant action, but a context in which it can ripple outwards. Each one of us has an obligation to keep the ground fertile and ready for change.

- We have an obligation to the rest of the world and a responsibility for the future.

- Even when we are focusing on our local community we should never forget that we are also part of a global world.

- We also need an "art" of action and so we should not forget how important artists can be in an organization or community. Artists often think in different ways so why not invite them onto boards and into organizations?

The emphasis was therefore on the personal but within the context of the global, or personal relationships and the importance of community, on ways of honouring individuality and spirit, on our sense of relationship to the land and on ensuring empowerment.

I was also left with some anecdotes. One concerned a man of 89 whose wife was just two years younger. He needed to buy a new car but also felt that he had to make his own contribution to caring for the environment and so he bought a very expensive hybrid. At the age of 89 maybe he would only drive that car for another year or two. In some ways it made no sense to make such an expensive investment in a new car. On the other hand that story had an enormous impact on other people and caused them to question their own travel habits. So a tiny action was given the opportunity of spreading outwards.

Before I left Calgary I was invited to a radio talk show. Inevitably the topic moved to that of Gentle Action. Some people phoned in to explain about a person or action that had deeply affected their lives. Then Pauline McCormick phoned in to tell me what happened when she went to London with her sister. She was on the underground and noticed all the passengers with their heads buried in newspapers or just staring blankly into space. Pauline began to smile and look around at everyone to the point where her sister said, "What are you doing? You look crazy." But Pauline replied, "I'm going to try to make someone smile." And sure enough in the end a young man in dreadlocks grinned back at here. What is more, when he was leaving the train he came over and hugged her.

It was a very tiny gesture. But what did it do to that man? How did it change his day? And what was his attitude to other people that day, did he pass something on to them? What if each one of us made a tiny gesture of recognition, help or friendship to a stranger? How would that spread out into the world?

Gordon Shippey, whom we have met several times in this book, has sent me another example; this time of an art student who noticed that the CCTV and loudspeaker system in her city centre had a depressing effect on people. In response she began to put up pictures of babies' faces, smiling and laughing. Naturally the local authority removed the pictures but people then began to ask why the faces had been taken down and even contacted the local press and radio stations to say that they had felt happier when they had those faces to look at. As Gordon comments, it was a very small thing indeed, but what if people really do feel that little more happy, and what happens when they go home to their partner or children or parents with a good feeling inside. "Just think," he writes "all kinds of events like new friendships, creation of a new life, new job, etc. can spring from such a simple act whether it is a smile or a picture of one!"

So let's end this book on a smile.

Conclusion

The idea of Gentle Action occurred to me back in the 1980s when I lived in a capital city and saw what was going on in the organizations around me, and when I read the newspapers and watched the television news to learn what was happening in the world. But unlike the other books I have written this one took a long time to see the light of day. Maybe because it seemed so obvious that so many of our institutions, plans and policies were on the wrong track, or based on erroneous assumptions, so why bother to write about them? On the other hand I couldn't help noticing people's strong positive response when I happened to mention the term Gentle Action.

So what are the conclusions of this book? That each one of us, in our daily lives with family, friends, community, work, vacation and travel is part of a complex system. Or rather that we are a part of a rich "system of systems" that interlock, nest, connect and feedback into each other. We are part of an ecology and ecologies involve a rich and diverse variety of subsystems—trees, plants, grasses, insects, animals, birds, fungi, worms and everything else that makes up the natural environment. Each one of these systems, each individual member feeds off the whole and, in turn, must contribute to its well-being.

In our case the ecology of our lives includes the natural environment, the earth itself, the marketplace, schools, transport systems, businesses and all the richness of human society. Thanks to the insights of chaos theory we have come to acknowledge that these systems can be incredibly robust in some directions, yet sensitive and delicate in others. We may have intellectual and technical knowledge of certain aspects of the system that is our lives, and important tacit knowledge about others. We may hope for a sense of certainty about the world yet must learn to live with a degree of uncertainty. We once sought to control the world around us but now have learned the inherent limitations of our desire for control.

And so we come to terms with our environment, we learn how to live in harmonious ways within our complex system of worlds. The problem arises when we begin to step outside our immediate world and enter into a new territory, at times uninvited, at times with the missionary zeal to "set things right", "improve the situation" or "teach the locals a better way to do things". Those are the extreme cases, situations we have explored in this book.

If there is anything to be drawn from this book it is that we must always be respectful of the situations in which we find ourselves, we must tread softly, we must follow that motto of the medical profession to "do no harm". We must learn to listen to people and listen to what systems are trying to tell us so that our actions may be more gentle and more creative. One way we may achieve a change of perception, I have suggested, is through a form of highly watchful "creative suspension". If we can truly be present to a situation, without the constant need to act out our desire for intervention, then maybe we and the institutions and systems of which we are members will themselves become more creative and flexible. Maybe they will begin to model or reflect within themselves the complex realities of the systems in which they are embedded. Maybe they will learn how to take a more appropriate action, one that flows out of the systems itself rather than something imposed from outside.

Taoist philosophy has its *wu-wei,* which could be thought of as a way of acting but without "taking action", in the sense of effort. The tree grows, water runs downhill, the moon circles the earth. Likewise in Gentle Action we can "go with the flow"; or rather each of us can make a tiny ripple—we can cause someone to smile, for example. And if these ripples begin to interact in a coherent way then we create Russell's great soliton wave, a wave that can move through society and teach a population to read and write, transform an inner city or even create an entirely new city in the pampas, or set political prisoners free.

❧ Reflections on Chapter 7

1. What effect has reading this book had on you? Are there some things you would choose to do in a different way? If so, what are they? What new steps do you intend to take?

2. Do you know of examples of Gentle Action? If so please share them with us.

3. Are there ways in which Gentle Action could be used in your workplace, community or social group?

4. How could Gentle Action be used nationally and internationally? If you have a definite idea in mind then what can you do about it and do you believe that one person can make a difference?

5. If you give to charity, or work as a volunteer, do you know exactly how the money is spent and how much goes to the deserving cause? Many agencies are doing very important work, so in addition to giving a donation also try to find out a little about them, become a participator.

6. Is there a particular case you know about that would benefit by microphilantropy?

7. What can you do to make a change in your community?

Don't forget to visit www.gentleaction.org.

Notes

1. Discussions with Dr. Shantena Sabbadini who is making a new translation of *Lao-Tzu*.

2 Alan Borer, *The Essential Joseph Beuys* (Cambridge, MA: MIT Press, 1997).

A brief biography can be found on Liverpool's Walker Art Gallery website: www.walkerart.org/archive/4/9C43FDAD069C47F36167.htm. His work can be seen at www.artcyclopedia.com/artists/beuys_joseph.html.

3. Satish Kumar, conversation with the author.

4. The birth of Amnesty and its effects can be found in an article in *The Observer* newspaper for February 27, 2005.

5. Lech Walesa, *The Struggle and the Triumph: An autobiography* (New York: Arcade Publishing, 1994). A short biography of Walesa can be found on the Nobel Prize website at http://nobelprize.org/nobel_prizes/peace/laureates/1983/walesa-bio.html See also http://www.cnn.com/SPECIALS/cold.war/kbank/profiles/walesa/.

6. Erik H. Erikson, *Gandhi's Truth: On the origins of militant nonviolence* (Gloucester, MA: Peter Smith, 1994)

7. Interview in *Vanity Fair*, July 2007.

8. See the Peace Camp's website: http://www.greenhamwpc.org.uk/.

9. Greenham Common Women's Peace Camp, 1981-2000, BBC News On-Line Monday, November 29, 1999.

10. Gordon Shippey in conversation and via a series of email communications.

11. Article in the *Daily Mail*, March 10, 2008.

12. Hassan Fathy, *Architecture for the Poor: An experiment in rural Egypt* (Chicago: University of Chicago Press, 1973) Aspects of Fathy's story were also told to me by my friend, the artist Siraj Izhar who spent time with Fathy in Egypt.

13. Edy Korthals Altes, *A Heart and Soul for Europe* (Assen, The Netherlands: Van Gorcum, 1999).

14. *To Serve the Present Age: The Brethren service story* , ed. Donald Durnbaugh (Elgin, IL: The Brethren Press, 1975) and an email exchange with Judy Glick-Smith, the granddaughter of M. R. Zigler and with Mary Flanagan, a NY representative of Heifer.

15. Alan Weisman, *Gaviotas: A village to reinvent the world* (White River Junction, VT: Chelsea Green, 1980).

16. Muhammad Yunus, *Banker to the Poor* (New York: Public Affairs, 2003).

17. Jurriaan Kamp, *Small Change: How $50 can change the world* (New York: Cosimo Books, 2006).

18. Correspondence with Christine Davis Egger.

19. See the Paolo Freire websites at www.paulofreire.org and www.paulofreireinstitute.org. Also discussions with Maureen Doolan who helped to set up the Ottawa-based adult literacy volunteer program, *People, Words and Change*, in part based on Freire's approach.

20. The story of Handsome Lake can be found in F. David Peat, *Blackfoot Physics* (Grand Rapids, MI: Phanes Press, 2002).

21. See a discussion of training in estimating volume, weights and the size of irregular objects in V. Field, *Piero della Francesca: A mathematician's art* (Yale: Yale University Press, 2005).

22. From my personal experience.

23. Discussions with Therese and a visit to her program when it was based in Missoula, Montana. See also the "Chalice of Repose" website: http://chaliceofrepose.org and her book *Transitus: A blessed death in the modern world* (Mt. Angel, OR: St. Dunstan's Press, 2001).

Pari Publishing is an independent publishing company, based in a medieval Italian village. Our books appeal to a broad readership and focus on innovative ideas and approaches from new and established authors who are experts in their fields. We publish books in the areas of science, society, psychology, and the arts.

Our books are available at all good bookstores or online at **www.paripublishing.com**

If you would like to add your name to our email list to receive information about our forthcoming titles and our online newsletter please contact us at **newsletter@paripublishing.com**

Visit us at **www.paripublishing.com**

Pari Publishing Sas
Via Tozzi, 7
58045 Pari (GR)
Italy

Email: info@paripublishing.com